Glory Street
and
Oblivion Avenue

A year in the lives of two brothers,
from the dawn of email

Kevin Pufall and Reagan Pufall

Copyright © 2021 Kevin Pufall and Reagan Pufall

Cover design by Kevin Pufall

All rights reserved

No part of this book may be reproduced, or stored in a retrieval system, or transmitted in any form or by any means, electronic, mechanical, photocopying, recording, or otherwise, without express written permission of the publisher.

Some names have been changed by request.

ISBN 978-0-9714486-2-9

*For our children, who left email behind but
continue to make our lives a delight.*

Contents

Fonts vii
Preface ix
1. September 1995: Message in a Bottle 1
2. October 1995: Carpe Diem 12
3. November 1995: Little Witch 46
4. December 1995: MacGyver, Jr. 68
5. January 1996: Spontaneous Long Impassioned Message 79
6. February 1996: Kick the Can 137
7. March 1996: Somewhere in the Center of My Torso 156
8. April 1996: Truth du Jour 167
9. May 1996: "How ironic, Superman" 182
10. June 1996: A Marvelous Time 206
11. July 1996: Maybe in My Next Life 211
12. August 1996: What Not to do When You're Depressed 221
13. September 1996: The Hulk 242
14. October 1996: Emotional Chrysalis 247
Afterword 249

Fonts

The fixed-font look of the original emails was an obvious and tempting choice, but it turned out to be less readable than desired. We also thought that it would be helpful to readers to be able to visually distinguish between the authors of the messages. Our solution was to use Times for Reagan and Calibri for Kevin. However, there are a few places, such as those involving emoticons and other images created from text characters, where the original look and spacing are crucial to the effect. In those cases, `Courier` is the font.

Preface

Kevin: It was a time of transition in the fall of 1995. I was 37 and living in Omaha, Nebraska. I had recently remarried, to Deborah, after an amicable divorce from Peggy, with whom I had two daughters, Sarah, 11, and Emily, 9. I had quit my job in the graphics department of a printing company and was living off savings to work on my first novel, a racy thriller titled Little Witch.

Reagan: I was 35 and had recently moved from Fargo to Bismarck, North Dakota with my wife Annie and our children Monica, 12, and eight-year-old twins Reagan Davis and Sabrina. We moved because I had been hired as an in-house legal counsel at the North Dakota Workers Compensation Bureau. It was an organization in crisis. It had been discovered that the Bureau was underfunded by about $200 million, meaning that there weren't enough funds to guarantee the payment of benefits to injured workers into the future. In reaction, the Bureau had started rapidly increasing premium rates each year, causing severe financial problems for many employers across the state. There were also serious shortcomings in the services provided to injured workers. I was part of a small group of people who took leadership positions in this deeply troubled organization at about the same time. We were beset by critics and adversaries on all sides; we operated under intense political scrutiny. No one thought we would succeed in turning it around.

Kevin: Reagan and I had always been very close, growing up, and had made sure to keep in touch after leaving home. Prior to email, the primary ways to communicate were by phone, which at that time had per-minute rates that could quickly add up to a big phone bill, and by letter, which was slow and required tedious effort. Still, we felt compelled to maintain contact. In addition to phone calls and letters, we sent each other envelopes and packages full of original cartoons, photographs, clippings, toys, and food items. Once, inspired by the McDonald's commercials that featured talking food characters, I bought a Quarter Pounder with cheese, affixed a pair of half-round puppet eyes, and mailed it to Reagan at college. It actually survived the trip rather well.

Reagan: The advent of email was a revelation: it was much easier, faster, and virtually free. Suddenly, sending "letters" was a breeze. It was like shifting from the Earth's gravity to the Moon's.

Kevin: I was already online via Prodigy and had been using its email feature to converse with a small group of friends. I had also, thankfully, developed the habit of keeping copies of my correspondence, on paper and on now-ancient diskettes.

Reagan: My job at the Bureau, which came with a desktop computer and internet access, gave me the ability to send and receive email for the first time. I immediately sent a message to Kevin.

1. September 1995: Message in a Bottle

Date: 9/15/95
From: Reagan
Subject: Message in a bottle

This is a test of the internet e-mail system. Had this been a real e-mail message, you would be reading something interesting or entertaining at this time. This has only been a test.

* * *

Date: 9/15/95
From: Kevin
Subject: to credit approval

Dude:

Does this mean we're "hacking a Net?" Or are we "surf-webbing?" Pretty dang cool, that's what we are. With my high-powered 2800 bps internal modem, it only took three and a half hours to "load down" your "E-message."

As you can tell, I'm right at home in the new "global subdivision." I've been "chattering" with many new "one-line" friends, a few of whom are actually not assholes.

A few tips from a veteran:

1. You can make punctuation marks mean things, like :) is a smiley-face turned on its side, % is an aerial view of a tennis match, $? means "I shouldn't have to remind you about the loan I gave you four months ago."

2. If you type in all upper case, it'll make all the geeks mad.

3. If you type with every other letter in upper case, the geeks will really have conniptions.

That is all.

* * *

Date: 9/24/95
From: Kevin
Subject: is unresponsive

Ideas for speeches* that you can throw in here and there:

1. "You, you're so fat, you're so fat your pants are enormous! They're so big, they're weird! They're made of so much material, they look like funny pants!"

2. "So, I walked into this store, and the sales moron says, 'Do you want to buy a hot water heater?' and I said 'You're so stupid! The water's already hot!' He was so stupid."

3. Take a drink of water. This will stretch things out a bit.

4. Mention your kids in a lighthearted manner. Many parents in the audience will identify with this.

5. You can pretend that there's a wall between you and the audience, you know, feel around with your hands and like that. Then you can bust through (pretend) with a hammer or something and talk to them through this hole.

6. Props are good, like a fishing rod or a diagram of some kind. Some places will do this for you.

7. If you quit before really reaching the end, and create a little suspense, they'll be likely to come back.

8. Here's for if they get restless: "Shut up! Hey, sit still, you! I'll bust you up good!"

9. You can make references to places you haven't been. They'll never know.

10. Have someone phone you while you're talking. That's another good time killer.

11. Wear vertical stripes and glasses with a hint of beige.

Reagan had begun giving speeches as part of his job with the North Dakota Workers Compensation Bureau.

* * *

Date: 9/25/95
From: Reagan
Subject: Re: is unresponsive

I may not be able to create humor, but I can still appreciate it. That was prime stuff, my eyes teared up and everything. My favorites are the big pants and talking through the imaginary wall.

One of the "interesting" things about having this incredibly high-resolution screen is that text and images whose size is determined by a certain number of pixels come out incredibly small. My internet e-mail messages look like legal notices in newspapers. Oops, I take it all back. There is an easy way to adjust font size, and I just did it. Now I can appreciate your amusing gags and gibes without eyestrain.

Strange, now that I can read them more easily they're not funny anymore. I guess you appreciate things more if you have to work for them.

If you get some huge glob of techno junk with this message, as you did last time, I will see if there is some way for me to avoid sending it.* As I said, when I was getting set up on this, the guy gave me the option of seeing that stuff on incoming mail or not, and there was a setting to not see it, so you may be able to screen it out on your end as well.

I am mildly horrified to have discovered, as I clicked around, a window bar dealie called "feelings." When you pull the menu down, you get three choices: Happy, Sad and Wink. You just click on them, and here's what you get: :-)   :-(;-). On my screen, it's pretty hard to discern Wink from Happy. You really have to look for it, which seems pretty ineffective to me.

I'm sure I'm not the first guy to do this:

=o	Scared witless
!:|	Hair parted on the right
#:|	Hair looks like Archie's
!%|	Glancing to the left
-^'	"Profile," or "Man Lying on Back, Gazing at Clouds"
&:|	Big pretzel on top of head
(:|	Bald, and he's OK with that
):(	Dismayed
(=o	Scared and dismayed
)=o	Scared and concerned, or scared and irked
<=o	So scared he wet his pants
>=(	Pretty steamed
<:)	Winsome
[:(	Frankenstein's Monster

September 1995: Message in a Bottle

```
(+|      Dead bald Cyclops

}=>      Satan

(:~|     Boxer, or Big Palooka, 3/4 view

 " " " "
( oo  )  Big upright guy with flattop, not much on his mind
  >
  _
```

Hey, this is fun! At least, for the guy doing it. I hope our computers have similar-looking fonts, so these don't come out looking incomprehensible.

See you later!

A "huge glob of techno junk" did indeed get sent at the end of every message – twenty lines of routing information, including such useful items as "MIME-Version: 1.0" *and* "Content-Type: TEXT/PLAIN; charset=US-ASCII"

* * *

Date: 9/25/95
From: Reagan
Subject: My lost message

Kevin, this morning I tried to send what I think was actually a pretty amusing message, of some length. I now have reason to believe that it simply vanished into the e-ether. Please advise.*

*I had good reason to be apprehensive. The first time I used a computer was to write my senior thesis at Haverford College. In the basement of the science building there was a room full of terminals connected to the college's mainframe. Progress on the thesis had fallen well behind schedule and on an evening just a couple of weeks before graduation I was among a group of fellow procrastinators typing away feverishly. Gradually we became aware of a conversation between a student and the teaching assistant; the student couldn't find his thesis. Eventually, the TA asked, "Did you save it?" to which the student replied, "What do you mean by 'save'." The rest of us were wondering the same thing; none of us had ever heard of "saving" something in a computer. The TA's conclusion – in a now completely hushed room – was that the thesis was probably gone forever, having been overwritten by other data. The student's friends more or less carried him out of the room. As soon as he was out of earshot, the rest of us were clamoring to be shown how to "save."

* * *

Date: 9/25/95
From: Reagan
Subject: Me again

I am sending this as an experiment to see whether my earlier misgivings were unfounded. Please bear with me.

* * *

Date: 9/25/96
From: Reagan
Subject: Me again, again

Yet another experiment. My apologies for the inconvenience.

* * *

Date: 9/26/95
From: Kevin
Subject: to some restrictions

Yes, I got 'em all! Including your very enjoyable "face" bit. I'm sure there's some kind of list or dictionary of such things out there, but I'm sure also that it doesn't have such gems as "scared and irked," "winsome" and "dead bald cyclops." My favorite: "big palooka, 3/4 view." If this is a non-creative period for you, you're going to be dynamite when you get to one.

There's still something blocking me up inside, something keeping me from succeeding. I'm going to see what I can do about it, let myself open up to possibilities. I may be out of contact for a little while, perhaps through the end of the week. No cause for alarm. I'll let you know how it goes.

* * *

Date: 9/27/95
From: Reagan
Subject: More thanks

I'm glad you received yesterday's message. My alarm arose from the fact that I had no messages in my "outbox." It seems that messages only stay in my outbox until they are successfully sent, which is about one second. This is in contrast to my past experience with in-house e-mail, in which outgoing messages are retained in the outbox until deleted.* For vain types such as myself, this permits one to call up one's particularly clever messages for one's own subsequent amusement. Actually, I wonder if you could mail a hard copy of the "faces" e-mail back to me at your leisure and convenience, as I wouldn't mind having a copy of it for reference if I might want to supplement it in the future.

Say! I just got the bottle of Moxie** in the cheese puffs canister. Come on . . . say it. I said say it, damn it! Oh forget it then, DON'T say it if you're going to be a poop about it!

Getting back to rationality, thanks for the vile drink! I'm touched. I think I will display it on my desk this week, then take it home, chill it, and drink it this weekend. Until then, if anybody hassles me, all I have to say is: "Hey buddy, you can't push me around! I'VE GOT MOXIE!"

Later, duh-hood.

*I didn't yet know the difference between "outbox" and "sent."

**Moxie is a soft drink with a challenging bitter flavor and the advertising tagline "You've got Moxie!" We had been introduced to

it during summer visits to our grandparents on the island in Maine on which our mother had grown up. At that time it was only available in New England but nowadays can sometimes be found in supermarket retro-pop sections. Kevin had taken it into his head to buy a bottle of it during a trip to Maine and mail it to me at my office. What he didn't know is that the Bureau was, at the time, such an object of animosity that we were frequently receiving bomb threats. When a cylindrical object wrapped in brown paper arrived in the mail, it created a security event. I was called to a meeting room where the package sat on a table, with everyone standing well back. Fortunately, I recognized my brother's distinctive handwriting and opened it, with the contents greatly amusing everyone.

* * *

Date: 9/27/95
From: Reagan
Subject: E-mail heaven

I was just sitting here working and it hit me that I can send you a message whenever I want, on a whim, and I thought, "Wow, cool."

Just wanted to share that with you.

Do I really tie up your computer for three hours every time I send a message, or were you just lying about that for humorous effect?

* * *

Date: 9/28/95
From: Reagan
Subject: A wee little joke

Q: What's the worst thing you can call a man?

A: A microsoft male.

I made it up myself! Just now!

* * *

Date: 9/28/95
From: Kevin
Subject: to the whims of his master

Yeah, well I'M a "microsoft male," "pal," and I'm not "laughing." Well, maybe a "little."

Yes indeedy, I have a copy of your funny comedy thing and will send it "soon." Also, yes, I was lying for funny comedy effect with the three hour bit. It's just interesting how quickly we become used to the idea of instantaneous responses to our actions on the computer. Waiting for more than a couple of seconds brings on finger-tapping tedium.

But I do need a faster modem. Much faster.

Also, also, "I just got a bottle of Moxie in the cheese puffs canister." So there.

* * *

Date: 9/29/95
From: Reagan
Subject:

Your subject lines are very funny. It's a good schtick, my friend! Frankly, as I can't come up with a schtick of my own for them, I'd just as soon skip that entry. I find myself staring at that little space with no idea what to enter. It inhibits the free flow of "at a whim" communication that e-mail seems so suited for. However, it seems that I can't send a message unless it has a subject. I'm going to try sending this one with a subject entry consisting of a space. If that fails, I might try "a." So if you get puzzling and brief subject entries, you'll know why.

Re: our phone conversation. I like your idea. Not, "What changes to my character could I make that would enable me to do the work on my desk, and how can I make them?" Instead, "I will do this work on my desk now (I wonder if this will have an effect on my character?)" Is that kind of it?

{?-| English guy, hair parted in the middle, with monocle.

* * *

Date: 9/30/95
From: Kevin
Subject: is suspicious and abusive

FFFFFFF:-) Guy wearing tall hat made out of "F"s

Hey, I'm getting the hang of this!

I think I'll save further "character change" discussion for our next phone conversation. It'll work better in a more interactive environment. But, yes, that was the basic idea.

Some potential Cub Scout activities:*

1. Stomp Your Pal. Remember when you'd get really mad at me and jump up and down on me while I was on the floor? This would be a great tension reliever.

2. Rat Chase. It wouldn't cost much to buy a small rodent for each meeting and let the kids chase it around the house. Whoever catches it takes it home!

3. Fart Flamethrower. I've never done this, and I feel I've missed something.

4. Scab Collection. Mount and display. Neatness counts.

5. Belch for Distance. How far down the block can they stand and still "call an audible"?

6. Face Painting. Not the sissy kind. Here, face = paintbrush.

7. Chaotic Racing Around and Hollering.

8. Home Haircut. Done solo or with a partner (blunt scissors best for this age group).

Reagan had recently become the den leader of the Cub Scout pack that his son had joined at the start of the school year.

2. October 1995: Carpe Diem

Date: 10/3/95
From: Kevin
Subject: is under surveillance

Hey, I came up with a "schtick" for you for the subject line. You just put in things like "algebra" and "history," like school subjects. With college courses, you could go on indefinitely! Such as Pre-Columbian Artifacts and so on. You're welcome. <(A little bit of interactivity)

I saw a '96 car preview in the paper and thought of you, especially when I saw the BMW Z3 Roadster. Whoa, momma! Have you seen it? Does it make you throb with excitement? Other random comments: Looks like a nice restyling on the Chrysler minivans and some thoughtful feature-adding. Taurus looks a lot like all those other big, roundy cars these days, which is not a bad thing. It's a lot better than when all the big cars were boxy and butt-ugly. Civic doesn't look as distinctively Civic-ish anymore. Mercedes E320 ($41,000), looks interesting. Know anything about it? Chrysler Sebring: Chrysler just keeps making good-looking cars! Taurus Wagon: looks weird & funky, like something was grafted onto the back of the sedan. I think I like it, but I wonder how well you can see out of it. Plymouth Breeze: sure as hell beats the K-cars! GMC Savana: Holy shit! In case you haven't seen one, I'll just say . . . "Seats HOW many?!"

***

Date: 10/3/95
From: Reagan
Subject: RE: is under surveillance

That was a very "nice" idea for a subject line schtick, but I've come up with a "better" one: All my messages will be replies to yours, thereby recycling your schtick right back at you buddy.

I think the BMW Z3 Roadster is hot stuff. Have you seen a side view? It has an unusually long hood, which should be awkward but is strangely compelling, a la the old Jaguar E Types. Is it worth 10,000+ more than a Miata? We'll see. I also like the looks and features of the new Chrysler minivans, although I'm sorry to see the high-teens price segment now empty. The new Chryslers look as good as the Villager and have more interior room. If Annie gets a job soon, we will be comparison shopping, and I'll keep you posted.

I want to criticize Ford for its conservative styling updates on the Taurus, but I'm not sure that would be valid. Here's the scenario: they grab a lot of attention and a big market share with bold and radical styling and half decent design and build quality. Then they bring quality up to good-enough-for-Americans and build a loyal customer base. Then they do a real conservative redesign, keeping their repeat business. Now they do a nice freshening, enough to make the car interesting for people looking for a standard issue sedan. All the while, they sell the things by the bucket. Meanwhile, everybody else is copying them (and Audi), and as you say the whole car market just looks a lot nicer than the grim box-o-rama days of the '70s and '80s. All in all, some pretty good decision making.

It seems to me that Honda lost its styling edge one or two restylings ago. I have never understood why they made the Acuras so bland-looking. Even the NSX: "It's the best car in the world, at a reasonable price, why aren't they selling better?" Because they look like the answer to a styling school challenge to try to make a car look simultaneously like a Ferrari and a family sedan, that's why.

The new Mercedes, across the line, are cheaper and better than the previous models. This, by the way, is a terrific time to get a two- or three-year-old Mercedes at an unheard-of low price, for just that reason.

Sebring looks great, goes OK, I'm keeping my eye on the convertibles for price and performance.

The Taurus Wagon seems to be Ford's sop to those who have been complaining about the conservative restylings of the sedans. It will be interesting to watch sales. At least it's better looking, and a much better deal, than Toyota's bizarre Camry wagons, and Honda's dull and uselessly tiny Accords.

The Breeze and the Savana are not known to me. Sounds like the Savana may have been inspired by the cult-hit mammoth Land Rover 110 and the hot selling restyled Suburban. The Rover was supposed to seat eleven, although that's hard to picture, unless it was 3, 3, 3 and 2 in fold down jump seats in back.*

I agree Chrysler is the styling champ over the last three years. Before that it was Mazda, to my eyes, but fat lot of good in did them. Why can't Honda style cars? It's become the Toyota of the '90s: good, pricey, and dull.

I have an irrational desire for a four door Suzuki Sidekick. It's cheap, has the compact looks I like, is useful in the winter, and has good build quality. Only drawback: it's not a Miata.

Had my first Cub Scout Den Meeting last night. Tougher than anticipated. More info to follow.

I now know that the Land Rover 110 came with various seating options. To get 11 people into it, the configuration would be two in the front seats, three on a middle bench seat, and then six more squeezed onto two inward-facing wall-mounted bench seats in the back. Pre-internet, you couldn't simply look this sort of thing up, as I did just now.

* * *

Date: 10/3/95
From: Reagan
Subject: Mr. Schtickless

I have an idea for a short story for you. You write about somebody doing something ordinary or having a common experience, but in describing what the person does and how he reacts to what is happening to him you subtly bring forth every aspect of life and human nature.

I really think this could be a successful story idea. I wonder why it hasn't been used before? Alternatively, you could have him do or experience the same sort of thing, except instead of the meaning-of-life-nature-of-humans thing you could put in a bunch of intrusive sexual and violent stuff, or you could adopt maybe a real cynical attitude or just make it really hard for the reader to understand what is supposed to be happening. Those angles might work too, I don't know.

Hey, if I had a big hat made of "F"s I'd be grinning too!

* * *

Date: 10/4/95
From: Kevin
Subject: to credit approval

Today's quote (from the Weather Channel's live coverage of Hurricane Opal):

"As you can see, we can't see anything here."

* * *

Date: 10/5/95
From: Kevin
Subject: to availability

A fun fragment from the book (What's in all caps would be underlined. What's in parentheses would be in italics):

> She looked into his eyes. "Welcome home, Wesley" she said, warmly and sincerely.

A twinge went through him, then a quiet sigh. "Thanks, sweetie. You do make me feel at home. You're very good to me."

"And you're very good FOR me. I needed someone like you in my life, someone who knows about life, about what's important." (Someone old. Someone who doesn't take erections for granted anymore.)

"I sure needed you. You're so full of life, adventure . . . you're so beautiful."

"So are you. You're the most beautiful man I've ever met." (You need to get out more.)

* * *

Date: 10/5/95
From: Kevin
Subject: to occasional lameness

Re-reading last night's "fun fragment," I realized how lame it was taken out of context. I've just been having a great time writing during the past week or so, very productive, spending a lot of time on it and very focused. I wanted to share some of that with you, but it's hard to find a short segment that stands alone. There's another scene with Mark (the slimy lech), but I'm reluctant to send potentially offensive stuff using this medium, not knowing how private it is.

Anyway, I wanted to save you the trouble of saying "Hey, Kev, that was lame! Send something more offensive, prying eyes be damned!"

That's just the kind of thoughtful literary genius that I am.

* * *

Date: 10/6/95
From: Reagan
Subject: RE: to availability

Actually, I didn't think it was lame at all, I thought it was good. I like the italicized "inside the mind" angle. The only problem with having the passage out of context was that it was not clear whether the last italicized phrase was supposed to be Wesley's thought or the woman's thought. I thought only Wesley's thoughts were being revealed to the reader, but that last thought seemed to be in her mind rather than his, unless it was supposed to be what he was thinking she was probably thinking. If her thoughts as well as his thoughts are being revealed, it seems you could have a hard time sustaining a mystery regarding her nature, and you may want to use another typeface.

Anyway, I enjoyed it and liked it.

Here's a sample of MY writing taken out of context for your enjoyment:

> You may request that subpoenas be issued to compel witnesses to attend the hearing and bring evidence to the hearing, pursuant to section 28-32-09 of the North Dakota Century Code. However, you will have to pay the witness fees and costs unless you get approval in advance. The Bureau will pay the cost of making its own experts available for cross-examination under certain circumstances. You may choose to have an attorney represent you, but the Bureau will only pay your attorney fees if you win. You will have the right to appeal the decision of the administrative law judge to district court.

Actually, I think that your writing is, at least on some level, somewhat more interesting and entertaining than mine.

Regarding racy messages: my message goes straight from my terminal to your server, which is probably at your service somewhere, where it is stored until you retrieve it. Your messages go straight from your terminal to the Bureau server, which is in the basement, and my terminal checks for them every five minutes and calls them to my screen. If someone wanted to, they could access your messages on the server, but that does not seem likely. So in terms of mentally screening what you write: your messages are not routinely being read by others, but could be retrieved by others in the future if someone decided they wanted to.

The job is very demanding, and I am right now in a scrambling mode, not really feeling like I am in the driver's seat.* However, I believe I will be able to get back on top of things soon. Annie has one decent job offer and is also applying for a job here at the Bureau she would really like to get. Kids doing well, closed on the house, cats becoming less destructive, driving to Minot tonight to see Mom. All in all, a good moment in time. House still pretty chaotic, about two thirds unpacked now, the really ugly little work remains.

*This is really putting it mildly. My first few years in this job were one of the most challenging experiences I have ever had. For example, around this time I ended up preventing a group of angry protestors from occupying our office building, as they had done some months before I arrived. I certainly never expected to find myself standing in front of a door with sign-waving, chanting protestors marching toward me while being filmed by a television news crew. Fortunately, the situation was resolved peacefully. I didn't blame the protesters for being angry; many of their claims had been handled poorly and they had not received the support they deserved. What mystifies me now is why I didn't relate any of these remarkable experiences in my emails. I've just never been inclined to talk about the events of my workday, I guess.

* * *

Date: 10/9/95
From: Reagan
Subject: Rise and shine

The wit and wisdom of Bernie Taupin at 8:24 AM?

Regarding the trip to Florida, maybe you should give Annie a call at home and give her the dates. She will have a school calendar there.

Have you ever seen the sort of tribute to Nana that Emily wrote on tagboard in Minot? It's really exceptional. Next time I'm up there I will copy it down and send it to you, if you have not seen it before.

***

Date: 10/9/95
From: Kevin
Subject: to applicable sales tax

Umm, I didn't get the Bernie Taupin reference. However, I did recently pick up one of your old favorite albums, with some of the most inspired song lyrics of the rock era:

> Somebody went under a dock
> And there they saw a rock
> It wasn't a rock
> It was a rock lobster

I hope that you're keeping track of all these great character faces. I smell a publishing possibility there.

Yes, I saw the tribute.* I took it up there on one of my most recent trips. That little girl has some amazing things inside her.

Also, loved your "subpoena" excerpt. People are probably bringing suit just to get letters from you.

*Emily wrote this lovely tribute on poster-size tag board to her grandmother when she in fourth grade:

> My Nana Sally
> Loving, funny, loves antiques.
> Dreams of fantasy things and a loving world.
> Who wants to make up things and have fun.
> Who wonders if other people know how to have fun.
> Who fears nothing.
> Who likes dresses and grandkids.
> Who believes in life after death.
> Who wishes for peace and joy.
> Who would like to see her two kids young again.
> We love you.

* * *

Date: 10/10/95
From: Reagan
Subject: RE: to applicable sales tax

Regarding Bernie Taupin, yesterday I had a voice mail message that consisted of an excerpt of Elton John singing "Don't Let the Sun Go Down on Me." I rashly assumed it was from you. Now I'm bemused and perplexed.

* * *

Date: 10/10/95
From: Kevin
Subject:

I've been sitting here staring off into space, assuming that some sort of message would begin to suggest itself, and I'm getting absolutely nothing. It's not really causing me a lot of stress or anything, so I guess I just have nothing to say right now. Rest assured that as soon as I do think of something to say, I will say it in your direction with due haste.

* * *

Date: 10/11/95
From: Reagan
Subject: is staring blankly into space

I've been feeling that way a lot lately, and I ain't just talkin' about e-mail, bub!

=
=   o
=   : | Staring into space
=   o
=

* * *

Date: 10/11/95
From: Kevin
Subject: has no time to be creative

Nothing has changed it's still the same
I've got nothing to say but it's O.K.
Good morning, good morning . . .

* * *

Date: 10/12/95
From: Reagan
Subject: RE: has no time to be creative

I yam the walrus.

Yes, walrus and yam, a Thanksgiving tradition for many Americans, evoking all those warm and wonderful Thanksgiving holiday memories: Jai alai in the living room. Firing guns into the air at dusk. Greasing up the oldest member of the family with Crisco, or a dairy based alternative edible lubricating product. Where have those days of old gone? What were we thinking at the time? Were we all mindless zombies, living an exterior pretense of a normal life but actually under the control of some insidious hidden masters who gained, and then apparently lost, the secret of cultural mind control? And is our current society, obsessed with superficial sex and violence to the exclusion of any wholesome or refined pursuits, really any better than that robotic simulation of existence? Why do you ask? No why do YOU ask? What are you implying here, that I have some kind of split personality problem? No, why are YOU implying that? Stop it! Stop it! Do you truly believe that I don't see what you are doing? Hah! Get away from that keyboard now, before I

* * *

Date: 10/12/95
From: Kevin
Subject: is northbound in southbound lane

I yam feeling a little bit cautious here, not quite knowing who I'm addressing. But, whoever you are, I remembered that I actually did have something to say.

Last weekend, Deborah and I visited the home of yet another friend with a home nestled in the woods. We had some lunch and decided to stroll amongst the trees. We followed a gully to fairly large river, which was paralleled by railroad tracks. While we were exploring, we heard a train approaching, and I harkened back to the days when you and I would be at the train station and try to stay at the edge of the platform as the train arrived. I sat down in the grass a few yards from the tracks, while my more prudent wife stood farther off in the edge of the forest.

As the train got closer, I heard the most interesting sound coming out of the tracks. It reminded me of something I haven't been able to recall yet, but it was kind of like metallic lightning. The train was setting up some kind of resonance, and the sound got louder and more energetic as the train closed in. I was so fascinated by this that I missed what it was telling me: this train was coming at me full-bore, not slowing into a station. The engine swung around the curve and the train was on me like a hurricane before I could react. My first thought was "YES!!" and my second thought was "This thing could kick up a rock and send it right through my head at any moment!" at which point I rapidly made for the woods. We watched the whole thing pass, and as it receded there was that same sound ringing from the tracks, which quickly faded away.

An interesting note: I felt the tracks immediately after the train left and they weren't even warm to the touch, due, I guess, to the lack of friction the make trains so efficient and also so hard to stop.

* * *

Date: 10/13/95
From: Reagan
Subject: RE: is northbound in southbound lane

Cool.

I'm pretty fascinated by the fact that the tracks weren't warm. Somehow, even without much friction, I would have expected the tracks to be warm from the weight and motion. It just seems strange that such massive weight passing at such high speeds wouldn't generate some heat in the metal tracks.

How long has it been since you put a coin on some railroad tracks? I must try to remember to do that with the kids the next time we go up to Minot.

I couldn't help noticing how well-written your little essay on the train experience was. I hope you won't think I critique every e-mail message you send for writing quality, but it kind of struck me that I would have been quite satisfied to read that essay in a magazine or book that I had paid good money for.

I am being sent my father-in-law's grandfather's shotgun. I will then go hunting for pheasant and partridge. I will keep you posted.

* * *

Date: 10/15/95
From: Kevin
Subject: may be wearing a wig and false lips

Hey, I forgot to tell you about the great adventure I had recently! See, we were walking in the woods and it turns out we were near a big airport, and I remembered all of our foolishness on the runways in Minot, playing dodgejet . . . well, now I'm thinking I already told you about this.

* * *

Date: 10/16/95
From: Reagan
Subject: RE: may be wearing a wig and false lips

False lips, eh? So THAT explains why you and Mick Jagger are never seen together!

I am in a discontented mode. It seems we have simply transplanted our stumble-through-life lifestyle from Fargo to Bismarck. I am not interested in living this way. I want to be carpe-ing diems on a more or less per diem basis. More later, perhaps, when I don't have to go to the bathroom so badly.

Actually, I don't go to the bathroom badly. I actually do it fairly well.

* * *

Date: 10/17/95
From: Kevin
Subject:

I have a feeling that the "diems" business was clever and humorous, but I've forgotten what it means. Oh, all right, maybe I NEVER knew what it meant, Mr. Big Pants College Boy! Maybe you just wanted to RUB IT IN to your stoopmo, unemployed . . . well, I think just about anyone could fill in the rest of this limp comedy bit.

Sorry to hear that things are not . . . copacetic? Are things ever copacetic these days? Haven't heard it used in years.

Well, isn't THIS just the rockin' little message! May as well quit while I'm sideways.

* * *

Date: 10/17/95
From: Reagan
Subject: Was blank

"Carpe diem" means "seize the day." It is an exhortation to live fully and actively, rather than simply drifting through it passively. I actually did not learn that at my big pants college, but from the movie "Dead Poets Society." I wasn't all that crazy about the movie, but that one thing really stuck with me. Despite its superficial source, it still seems to be a powerful message, one I would like to follow much more than I now am.

I think things should be copacetic again. I find myself longing for values and experiences like "wholesome," "happy," "joyful," "innocent," and "enthusiastic." Why has our society so completely embraced the values of cynicism and decadence to the exclusion of these superior values? Why were we so eager to give up the possibility of feeling wholesome and joyful without having to feel embarrassed and self-conscious about it?

Well, I guess I'm in a bit of a serious vein this morning. I have to go to a seminar RIGHT NOW so I can't leaven this with parting humor. Later kadudelmeister.

* * *

Date: 10/17/95
From: Kevin
Subject: to rectal searches

Hmm . . . I put in the subject before reading the printout of your message, and now I'm thinking that it really doesn't fit well with your very accurate observations on current values. Well, I suppose with some stretch of the imagination one could picture an "enthusiastic" probe taking place if it was suspected that the probee was secreting something of great value.

Anyway, "carpe diem" . . . I do like that phrase and what it represents. I know that I do a lot more of that than I used to, but I could certainly develop the kind of internal dynamism that the phrase suggests much more fully.

Okay, here's some "parting" "humor": "Alright, Mr. Big Pants, drop 'em and part 'em, you're the probee du jour!"

* * *

Date: 10/18/95
From: Reagan
Subject: RE: to rectal searches

Well, that last line of yours was certainly a multi-referential tour de force. I'm still chuckling!

I find it somewhat interesting that "carpe diem" is translated as "seize the day." The word "seize" lends it a weighty and distinguished air. But how do we know that in its original use it didn't mean something more like "grab the day" or "snatch the day?" Just a nuance, true. However, it fits in with the solemnization of old arts of which I have grown suspicious. Classical music was the pop music of the royal class, for example, not some kind of stuffy "shut up, it's good for you" experience. Similarly, I doubt the Romans were always walking around portentously declaiming things. If "portentously" is even a word.

However, I actually prefer the "seize the day" translation, as for me it best conveys the message of the phrase.

Do you enjoy word origins? I sure do. It adds something to carpe diem, for example, to know that the bones in your hands are called carpal bones. Like a tarsier monkey is named after its elongated tarsal bones. That is how I remember that carpal bones are in your hands while tarsal bones are in your feet: the tarsier monkey has greatly elongated feet (or ankles, or something down around that area somewhere, anyway).

I wonder why I so readily remember something like that, that I read many years ago in a science magazine, when I can't remember the names of the people I work with, or the names of the claimants whose files I have worked, or to attend meetings or lunch date. The thing is, if I had to choose, I would choose to remember as I do now. It is embarrassing and awkward to be forgetting regular stuff all the time, but life is more interesting with all these other facts cross-correlating in the back of my mind all the time.

As another example, why do so few people remember what to do in case of a fire, as we have discussed? There was recently an article in the paper here. Several people had been killed as follows: they were driving along, an oncoming car crossed into their lane, they swerved left into the oncoming lane to avoid the car, the oncoming car simultaneously swerved back into its lane, and the cars then collided head on. The message of the article was: always swerve to the right, in other words, take the ditch. Now I would remember to do that! It's right there in my mind. I learned it in Driver's Ed, I saw the logic, and that is what I would do. But if you think about it, most people would probably swerve left.

I'm not saying I'm better than anyone else. For example, I have a pretty lousy memory. It's just that there is a pattern here of some kind, and I wish I understood it better.

Anyway.

Here is my e-mail experience. I come in in the morning and start logging on my various applications. It takes a while. Internet e-mail is the third application I log onto. I get an icon that looks like a country mailbox. If I have incoming mail, I get a little beep, the little red flag on the mailbox goes up, and the mailbox door opens to show a letter inside. That makes me happy, because to date that means it's probably from you. The purpose of the system is communication with our two outside law firms, but one of them, my old firm, isn't hooked up yet, so I haven't been using it for that much yet.

* * *

Date: 10/19/95
From: Kevin
Subject: to diminishing returns

Like you, I occasionally have to remind myself that history is the story of living people in a dynamic world, not dead people in a book.

Musing on your "carpe diem" comments . . . is it possible that hundreds of years from now someone will find a personal rallying cry in "Be all that you can be" or "Just do it?"

And the Romans . . . yes, there was probably a great deal of lively foolishness going on, but it's certainly possible that "portentous declaiming" was admired and the preferred method of public speaking during some periods. Think of the history of U.S. political speechmaking, or of the Nazi and Fascist rallies . . . is any of this making sense?

Anyway, speaking of U.S. politics, I have it in mind that one of the things I'm going to do when the book is done is to find out more about William Jennings Bryan. His name has popped up a few times and I'm curious. My very sketchy current impression is that he was the worst sort of American political animal, a "populist" appealing to the shallowness and ignorance of those who kept him in power. Are you acquainted with his career?

Interesting thoughts on memory, and I feel much the same way: it would be convenient to have a better memory for daily details, but I value more highly the creative uses to which mine is apparently dedicated.

My e-mail experience: Usually, I check it in the evening when I sit down for my night-shift writing. I log onto Prodigy, which is tedious because I have such a slow modem. If I have mail, a small, crude picture of a letter appears at the bottom of the screen, and I am also excited because the message is nearly always from you. If it's not, it's advertising.

```
                              MMMMMMMM
                              M        M
                MMMMMMMMMMMMMM          MMMMMMMMM
           MM    MM           M  MMMMMM          MM
         MM        MM         M  M                 MM
MMMMMMMMMMMMMMMMMMM           M  M                  MM
M====                     MM  M  M                  MM
M                ======  M    M  M                   M
M                ======  M    MMMM                   M
MMMMMMMMMMMMMMMMMMM                                  M
       MMMMMMMMMMMMMMMMMMMMMMMMMMMMMMMMMMMMMMMMMMMMMMM
```

Let me know how this little work of art* comes out. As you may have seen on the hardcopy I mailed to you, your messages frequently print out here with repeated letters and shifted lines, causing a distortion in some of the character faces you've done. No big deal, just curious.

*It's supposed to be the AOL mailbox icon with the flag raised and a letter coming out the door. If you lean back and squint you can kind of see it. At the time, the icon and the chipper male voice saying "you've got mail" were so well known that a very popular movie was made called "You've Got Mail" starring Tom Hanks and Meg Ryan.

* * *

Date: 10/19/95
From: Reagan
Subject: RE: to diminishing returns

Wrote reply to your message, somehow erased it in printing it, will try again later, no time now.

* * *

Date: 10/19/95
From: Kevin
Subject: to explosive decompression

Good, 'cause I have no time to read it! Ha Ha!

* * *

Date: 10/20/95
From: Reagan
Subject: Just carpe the diem

Here is the message you should have received yesterday.

Wow, you are running the "subject" schtick out much longer than I imagined you could! And it's still funny!

It's interesting, that if you can take them out of their advertising origins, both "be all that you can be" and "just do it" can give you a lot to think about. If they were quotes from some stirring essay or poem by a notable figure, either one could be taken at least somewhat seriously as an item of personal inspiration.

"Seize the day" and "just do it" are similar messages. I prefer "seize the day" because it does not carry quite the connotation of unthinking action that "just do it" does. Sloth and inaction are a big problem in our society, but it seems to me that another big problem is that people plow through life – whether achieving, wasting time, playing, or whatever – in an unreflective way, taking for granted the mores and values that surround them. "Just do it" strikes me to some extent as a call to vigorous but undirected activity that could well be, and in fact is likely to be, ultimately pointless. The call to action is good, but the call to "just" act is not.

"Seize the day" urges one to consider how the day can best be seized, to evaluate what the best and highest use of the day would be, and THEN to act.

I'm still thinking about "be all that you can be," but it seems to me there is fruitful ground for thought there.

Nice comment on the declaiming Romans.

Your hazy impression of Bryan matches mine, as does your curiosity about him. Keep me posted. It's interesting, isn't it, that there are some important and historical figures who never seem to get a final verdict. Bryan had a large and loyal following for many years, and was a hero to many Americans. Although his image seems somewhat questionable now, as reflected in your comments, I don't think there is anything close to a consensus on him at this time. In part, that may be because the issues he was most involved in, like free silver, just sort of faded away, rather than being resolved with some finality, as being pro- or anti-slavery or Naziism were.

I will try to recreate here an interesting political insight I once learned. People often think of political ideology as a one-dimensional continuum, from "left" to "right" with the mainstream consisting of the center of that continuum, from "liberal" to "conservative." However, it may be more fruitful to think of ideology in two dimensions:

```
| liberal   | conservative |
|------------------------|
| populist  | libertarian  |
```

I may not get this quite right, but here goes: Left of the vertical axis is government intervention in the economy (mainly in a wealth spreading or equalizing mode). Right of the vertical axis is government economic "non-intervention" (which may actually be government enforcement of the rules of an economic system favoring the wealthy few). Above the horizontal axis is government non-intervention in cultural or moral choices (this is an old analysis, nowadays liberals have gone beyond opposing government enforcement of "traditional" or "repressive" values to the point of favoring government intervention in favor of "politically correct" values). Below the horizontal axis is government intervention in cultural or moral choices (although the conservative side has been so thoroughly defeated in recent decades, they are now really in the position of trying to make up lost ground by opposing government intervention favoring "politically correct" values).

So populism could be seen as economically liberal but culturally conservative. Since this combination would be seen as unattractive in whole or in part, almost a worst of both worlds position, to most influential people in the political climate of the past twenty or so years, populism and populist issues have just seemed irrelevant.

Except, of course in North Dakota, where populism has dominated politics for about the last 90 years.

The other problem with populism, which you alluded to, is that most politicians who call themselves populists really aren't. They are ignorant demagogues who instinctively sense they will never be able to pass themselves off as intelligent or knowledgeable, but that they may be able to disguise their lack of brains and sophistication as being "a man of the people" and then preying on the people's paranoia, fear, and envy. This gives real populism a bad name, especially since there are so few real populist politicians around nowadays.

Your artwork looks a lot like my happy little mailbox! Nice job. I printed it.

* * *

Date: 10/20/95
From: Kevin
Subject: to carping the diem

Further thoughts on "Just do it." When I have seen that slogan over the years, I've read it as part of a statement like "No more excuses. No more whining. Just do it," the kind of thing a manager or commander might growl to his subordinates. Now, depending on a variety of factors, like the capabilities of the boss and the underlings and the circumstances in which the statement was uttered, the results can range from disastrous to triumphant. Thinking back to the Nazis again (I seem to do that a lot . . . the idea of having lived so close in time to that evil of historic proportions continues to amaze me) you can see that spectrum clearly, from the astonishing successes of Hitler's rise to power and the early military campaigns to one of the most crushing defeats ever recorded. From reading Speer's book, I came to understand that Hitler's "Just do it" approach was in large part responsible for all of it. In the beginning, a combination of capable underlings, current and potential German strengths, and weakness and disorganization among the future Allies allowed Hitler time and again to brush aside the concerns of naysayers and achieve startling results. He became so habituated to this pattern that later on, when there really were concrete impediments to success, he was unwilling to accept them as real and unable to adjust his plans to overcome them.

I must admit that I have often played the part of the defeatist in my lifetime, and have only recently begun to switch from "What's preventing me from doing this?" to "How can I accomplish this?" I learned a great deal during my years at Lancer* about getting things done. I learned that there are almost always strong, valid reasons for things to be going badly and further reasons why it would be difficult to change things for the better, and I was certainly capable of coming up with lots of those reasons. On the other hand, particularly since I worked a late shift all those years, I had to find ways of solving problems and fixing things on my own, and I discovered that I wasn't too bad at that, at least on a limited, practical level. I had more trouble coming up with workable, system-wide solutions to problems, either because I'm naturally less talented in that way or because I didn't challenge myself enough. But I did find myself cutting through the moaning of others and saying "Okay, let's just establish the situation and see how we can proceed from there."

It seems as though the central question is "Are you determined to succeed?" and, if so, to focus on the goal rather than the obstacles.

Thanks for the lesson in politics. I would like very much to have a long conversation about your political thoughts and knowledge, even if it is less of an interest to you than it used to be.

*Lancer Label was a printing company in Omaha where I had previously worked in the graphics department.

* * *

Date: 10/20/95
From: Reagan
Subject: A carp per diem keeps the dr. away

Now that I have that image in my mind of some impatient workplace superior barking "just do it," I don't think that phrase will ever seem quite the same to me again. While it is tiresome when people get real negative and get stuck on all the reasons something can't be done, managers who respond with a "just do it" type message are often, in my experience, assholes, not to put too fine a point on it. A better response might be something more like "figure out how to do it," or even "let's figure out how to do it."

I agree with your comments on result-orientation, or perhaps more aptly, achievement-orientation. I have found myself, now that I am in somewhat of a managerial or decision-making position, impatient with negative, obstacle-oriented thinking.

What I like about "be all that you can be" is that it makes you reflect on whether there is some whole dimension to yourself that you have not developed or even recognized. It is an invitation to reflect on facets of yourself, or abilities, that you may not have ever perceived, or that got left behind long ago in life. For example, should I take it for granted that I am not an adventurer or thrill seeker? Wouldn't my life be more full if I experimented with tapping into that part of myself? The phrase implies that achievement is not always linear progress down the road you're on, but can also be growing and developing along other roads as well.

I'm afraid that with politics I have very much developed a negative, obstacle-oriented outlook. I just hate everything I can see in politics now. I can't even stand to listen to them or read about them. I can only wonder if this will turn out to be one of those perceptual issues, and that a time will come when my perspective will shift and I will suddenly see the possibilities rather than the problems.

* * *

Date: 10/23/95
From: Kevin
Subject: to FCC regulations

Hey, bro'. Hope your week is off to a good start. I had a thought concerning politics and why I'm not all that fond of it: our old nemesis, word inflation. Nothing new here, it just came back into consciousness with a look at the newspaper and all the current accusations of extremism flying about.

Here's the Hunter S. Thompson quote on Muskie that I was telling you about:

Some of his top staff people considered him dangerously unstable. He had several identities, they said, and there was no way to be sure on any given day if they would have to deal with Abe Lincoln, Hamlet, Captain Queeg, or Bobo the Simpleminded . . .

* * *

Date 10/23/95
From: Reagan
Subject: Me and Monica*

Dear Uncle Fuzzy,**

How are you and Deborah doing? Tomorrow is my thirteenth b-day. I can hardly wait. This weekend I am having my party. I have already had my friends from Fargo up to visit. Tell Sarah I hope she had a great b-day. Can you send her E-mail address to me?

*Monica was in the office with me after hours to work on a school assignment, which was not unusual in an era when only about a quarter of US households had a home computer. We would soon get our first PC as a family Christmas present.

**About a year prior, Kevin had experimented with cutting his own hair using electric clippers. His first attempt left him with hair quite a bit shorter than intended, leading to the nickname. Although he had since grown it out, the name had stuck.

* * *

Date: 10/23/95
From: Kevin
Subject: is en route to the Chilean Embassy

Hi, Monica! Happy Birthday!

Thanks for the message! Deborah and I are doing great. Not too much to report—she goes to work, I write, I pick up Sarah and Emily, Deborah and I have dinner and I write some more. That's plenty for now.

Sarah had a terrific birthday party. Peggy and Carl got poolside rooms at the Holiday Inn and decorated one room for Halloween—spider webs, red lightbulbs, a screaming door mat, a snake in the toilet, etc., etc. Sarah and her guests spent the night in that room after pizza and swimming.

I will get her e-mail address. It would be great if you could exchange messages that way.

I hope your birthday and birthday party are a lot of fun, and I look forward to seeing my teenage niece soon.

Love,
Uncle Formerly Fuzzy

* * *

Date: 10/23/95
From: Reagan
Subject: RE: is en route to the Chilean Embassy

We are here at my office trying to finish one of Monica's homework projects, late at night the day before it is due, as is not unusual. Thanks for writing back!

* * *

Date: 10/24/95
From: Reagan
Subject: Most significant message ever

Your comment about word inflation was the most insightful and penetrating analysis I have ever read.

The word inflation bothers me too. That's one of the reasons I just can't stand listening to those people anymore, why I haven't watched TV news for about the last eight years or so. It's the word inflation plus that subtly dreadful way they all talk, that edge of phoniness and angle-playing that creeps into their voices, that tone that says, "I could say absolutely anything with this voice, anything at all, true or false, and some part of me will even believe it's true, and truthfulness gives me the edge I need to get reelected."

" " " " "
(' ') Plain Guy
 ‾

* * *

Date: 10/24/95
From: Reagan*
Subject: "snotnose"

Dear Uncle Fuzzy,

Thank you for the card.** My pony is doing fine. How is your pet turtle "Humorous" doing? Tell Sarah and Emily I enjoyed the card, and the money. Tell everyone I love them and miss them.

Your wonderful, witty, charming, funny, beautiful, and always modest niece,

Monica Pufall

And Monica, again.

**Birthday card to Monica from Kevin, Emily, and Sarah:*

> Dear Monica:
> How is my fine and wonderful niece today? Fine and wonderful, I hope. Your mom and dad tell me that you are obeying their every whim and desire and are a perfect daughter in every way.
> Congratulations on the astrophysics scholarship to M.I.T.! So unusual for such a young student. Gosh, I'm glowing with pride.
> And how is your pony, "Snotnose"? I know you were having a little trouble getting her housebroken, but stick with it. It's a real comfort to have someone to snuggle into bed with during those cold winter months.

I am fine and wonderful my own self. I just finished the ragweed harvest, and it looks like I'll have enough pollen to keep my eyes watering well into next summer.
    Love,
    Uncle Kevin

Dear Monica,
    how are you!? I'm fine. I just found out I'm in the challange reading group! I just finished my first swimming met and I got a blue ribbon. Well, I hope your having as good of a time as I am. I miss you!
    Love,
    Emily

Dear Monica,
    Merry Birthday. I had a good birthday myself at the Holiday Inn last Saturday. Merry Birthday and a happy New Year.
    Love,
    Sarah

* * *

Date: 10/25/95
From: Kevin
Subject: to irrational outbursts

Paragon Cable in New York recently began a new approach to customers with delinquent accounts. Instead of cutting off service altogether, which would create additional expense to restart when the customer paid up, Paragon merely fills those customers' entire 77-channel lineup with C-SPAN. Paragon said the project has been successful.

Tell Monica that I'm teaching Humorous a new trick called "Run Away." I put him on the floor and let Deborah's cat, Lily, into the room. Humorous is learning fast.

* * *

Date: 10/25/95
From: Reagan
Subject: Dear Mr. Peafowl

It bothers me a little that when I run Spell Check on my letters the suggested "correct spellings" for "Pufall" are "peafowl, peephole, and piffle." These are not distinguished alternatives.

I don't know if I have ever actually watched C-SPAN. A case could certainly be made, however, that 72 channels of C-SPAN would be worse than no channels at all.

Just LOVED your card to Monica. She thought it was really funny too, which is troubling.

* * *

Date: 10/25/95
From: Kevin
Subject: is frightening the nurses

I apparently have the same spell checker. This is a case where a No Alternative Found would be preferable. My last boss at Lancer spell-checked me name and came up with "puffball," which greatly amused her, and I was "Mr. Puffball" after that.

I really enjoyed doing the card. It was fun to realize that Monica is getting to an age where she can appreciate more grown-up forms of humor. I'm sure having fun with my girls these days.

More strangeness:

> A circus lion bit off a finger of a woman who scaled three fences and stuck her hand inside the cage to pet the animal. Lisa Fox, 31, told police she put her hand into the lion's cage at a downtown Indianapolis area used by the Ringling Bros. Barnum & Bailey circus. The index finger on Fox's right hand was severed and, "according to the police report, it was recovered and taken

to the hospital," police officer Mary Horty said. Fox was not charged in the incident.

I really wish that this story had included some kind of statement from Ms. Fox.

* * *

Date: 10/26/95
From: Reagan
Subject: Feeding the lions

It is amazing how hard people will work to injure themselves. It is also amazing how often, when people have exerted herculean efforts to do damage to themselves, they will then sue someone for not having made it even harder to damage themselves. I would not be a bit surprised if Ms. Fox sued the circus for not having higher fences, warning signs, etc.

"Failure to warn" is a big theory for legal recovery in the most unlikely cases. I can just see Ms. Fox's lawyer arguing that there should have been big signs all around the cage saying "Warning, don't stick any body parts in here, lions bite. Lion bites can result in death or serious bodily injury."

What I would like to ask Ms. Fox is: "Ma'am, at that point in time, what were you using for brains?"

Do you think circuses should really be dragging animals around in cages anymore? That seems like a cruel holdover from a less enlightened age at this point. Of course, I don't like circuses, which may color my thinking. Clowns have always repulsed me. It is absurd for trapeze artists and high wire walkers to literally risk their lives for the mild amusement of an audience which has seen better a hundred times on TV anyway. The seedy mock glamour veneer on the hobo lives the performers lead is depressing. I just think the whole institution has long outlived its time, and should quietly fade away.

* * *

Date: 10/27/95
From: Reagan
Subject: Seven screaming dizbusters

Did you use the plastic sheeting for walls in your haunted houses?*
Does your garage have a sheetrocked ceiling? If so, did stapling the plastic walls to the sheetrock hold up, or did you have some other method to fasten the walls up?

I have Annie's great-grandfather's shotgun. It's cool. Side by side double barrels. Pete's going to instruct me in shooting this weekend, with clay pigeons. I'll let you know how it goes.

Kevin had begun creating "haunted" mazes in his garage every Halloween, fashioning the walls of the maze out of black plastic landscape sheeting stapled to the rafters. I started doing the same for my daughter Monica's birthday parties, which were in October, and over the years we took the concept to higher and higher levels of complexity, enlisting our children to participate and adding features such as remote-control skeletons, strobe lights, fog machines, and scary sound effects, all operated out of central control booths.

* * *

Date: 10/30/95
From: Reagan
Subject: junk e-mail

I got my first internet junk-mail today, a "good luck" chain letter. I don't like chain letters. However, this one did have a funny part, which follows:

WHY ASK WHY?

1. Why do you need a driver's license to buy liquor when you can't drink and drive?

2. Why isn't phonetic spelled that way?

3. Why are there interstate highways in Alaska and Hawaii?

4. Do you need a silencer if you're going to shoot a mime?

5. Have you ever imagined a world with no hypothetical situations?

6. How does the guy who drives the snowplow get to work in the morning?

7. If the 7-11 is open 24 hours a day, 365 days a year, why are there locks on the door?

8. Why do they put braille dots on the keypad of a drive-up ATM?

9. Why do we drive on parkways and park on driveways?

10. Why is it that when you transport something by car it's called a shipment, but when you transport something by ship it's called cargo?

As an experienced internet "surfboarder" and long-time computer "hasher" you may have already encountered these. They made me laugh, anyway. These are culled from about 20 that came attached to the very lengthy chain letter.

* * *

Date: 10/30/95
From: Kevin
Subject: junk e-mail

I enjoyed the clever junk-mail list. My junk-mail seems to be limited to Prodigy-related advertising. I'm guessing that they don't allow outside "mailings," since this is a paid-for service, kind of like HBO.

Speaking of TV, I watched the Simpsons Halloween show. Man, do they pack in the action! There was a great nine-minute take-off of "The Shining," something that I would guess could easily have been stretched to fill the entire show.

I'm with you on circuses. For a long time it was just the clowns that gave me the creeps, but for many years the thought of going to one at all has repulsed me. I had the idea that I should take the girls to one (they may have seen one when they were very young), so that they'd have that experience before the circuses do finally fade away, but I'm thinking now that they can do without it.*

I do have some fond memories of going to the circus as a boy. It was one of the few times during the year that cotton candy was available, and we always came home with some cheap memento that we would enjoy until it fell apart.

* * *

Date: 10/30/95
From: Reagan
Subject: RE: junk mail

Greatly am I regretting that I missed the Simpsons Halloween special, which is consistently one of the best hours of TV in the year. My consolation: I carped the diem extensively this weekend.
Saturday AM: pheasant hunting with Pete, much fun.

Saturday PM: roast and eat yummy pheasant, begin work on haunted house with Monica.

Sunday AM: work at a FAST pace on haunted house.

Sunday PM: prepare for Cub Scout pack meeting (the big pack-wide Halloween party!) I had forgotten about, simultaneously finishing haunted house at EXTREMELY FAST pace.

Sunday evening: attend pack meeting in monkey suit* with Reagan, hastily improvised apple dunking game is big hit, take off early, run haunted house with twins which is also big hit with Monica's new friends.

I was on the go big time 16 hours out of each day. I have the good tired "I've used my body and mind to the fullest" feeling. And it all worked out beautifully despite coming just under the wire on everything.

Dead guy in a noose, pull operated, was a big new hit. Details upon request.

A few years earlier, our mother and Annie, both skilled at sewing, had created matching head-to-toe monkey costumes out of fake fur as gifts for Kevin and me. Monkeys were a theme in our lives: we had loved pretending to be monkeys as kids, clowning around and swinging from tree branches, and had jointly developed monkey characters that we used for many years in our cartooning. The suits proved quite useful, not just on Halloween but at many parties and events. We still have them and still use them.

* * *

Date: 10/31/95
From: Kevin
Subject: to sudden voltage surges

Please forgive me if my messages are irregular and uninspired for the next couple of weeks. I'm finally seeing an end to this project and am getting more and more focused on reaching that end. I've felt better and better about this life choice as I've gone along, and I'm feeling more positive all the time that I'm producing something unique and creative that actually stands a chance of being successfully published. I'm not claiming to be writing great literature, but I'd happily settle for the title of "published author."

At some point, soon, I hope, I'll be sending a draft of the book up there for you and Annie to read and critique. I've shown smaller portions of it to a couple of people and have gotten some very useful advice from them. I'm most interested in the comments of those people who are willing to be very honest about what they've read, both positively and negatively, and I know I can count on the two of you for that.

Congratulations on a successful and rewarding couple of diems. I'd like to hear more about this year's haunted house setup and the crowd reaction. I, too, have carped the diem by the nuts, and am planning to continue carping strenuously until . . . well, this can't lead anywhere good, so I'll leave it at that.

* * *

Date: 10/31/95
From: Reagan
Subject: Vivid imagery

"Carped the diem by the nuts." I love it.

I have noticed for the last week or two that you have seemed preoccupied and distracted, and that has actually given me a really good feeling. I feel that I am in touch with what is going on with you in terms of your focus, and it's great. I'm still surprised at how far along in the process you are, as I would have expected a week or two ago that you were still, let's say, toward the end of the beginning of writing the book, and that you would now just be entering into the long middle phase.

Anyway, just go ahead and do your thing, don't worry about maintaining any kind of steady communication stream with me.

3. November 1995: Little Witch

Date: 11/3/95
From: Kevin
Subject: felt a slight draft

Well, I just mailed the first draft of my book. I'd very much appreciate it if both you and Annie would read it and critique it. I'm open to any and all comments, positive and negative, concerning everything from spelling and word usage through plot and character to overall readability and clarity. Feel free to mark up the manuscript. I didn't print it out double-spaced because it just takes up too darn much paper.

Concerning length: I'm not planning for it to end up being a very long book, for a variety of reasons. I'm figuring that it's about 65% to 70% of its finished length at this point. If you have any doubts or questions on that point, I'd like to hear them.

I'd like to have it back when you're done, as I'd prefer not to have varying versions of the manuscript outside of my control. Also, you'll want to keep it out of the hands of the kids; it is very explicit.

In case this is sounding too dry and formal, I should say that I've never felt more creative in my life. It's been very rewarding just writing, and now adding the elements of sharing and discussing what I've written is putting another layer of pleasure on the process. I'm really looking forward to hearing from you.

* * *

Date: 11/6/95
From: Reagan
Subject: Fake book review schtick

I got your manuscript in the late Sunday mail, and stayed up all night reading it.

Positive comments/warm fuzzies:

>It was neatly typed.
>
>It had that certain je ne sais quoi.
>
>It had that certain "I don't know what."
>
>It had the faint musty odor of an old attic, a smell evoking an ineffable nostalgia for a past we can't truly remember and yet can never escape, and the haunting longing for the lost innocence of an age when despair was only a shadow of foreboding on the edge of our emerging consciousness.

Suggestions/criticisms/brickbats:

>The modern reader wants the wildlife element in his fiction, and will not feel he has gotten his money's worth without it. I recommend wildebeest, preferably a large, thundering herd of them, with foam-flecked mouths and wide rolling eyes.
>
>You need a photo on the back. Go shopping for a tweed coat and start practicing your smug, knowing expression in front of the mirror.
>
>Imbue the pages with a light scent of jasmine. Otherwise, the musty attic thing will have all your readers preoccupied with an ineffable longing for childhood.

The early returns are in:

>"Many misspellings . . . Peafowl needs to use a spell checker on his text."

"Filled me with an ineffable nostalgia for childhood . . . musty odor clung to my hands for days."

"Piffle has . . . has [written] . . . a text."

"For some reason I can't quite put my finger on, this book reminded me of The Sun Also Rises."

Authentic comments will follow, after I have actually received and read it.

* * *

Date: 11/7/95
From: Kevin
Subject: had a drink and left without incident

I'll practice responding to my critics:

"Fuck you! Fuck you! Yeah, you too, buddy! Eat me! Kiss my ass! You wouldn't know good writing if it crawled up your nose and laid eggs in your brain that hatched into horrible alien things that burst out of your skull in a spray of blood, bone, and tissue!"

I really enjoyed your note. It was the laugh-out-loud and reread it and laugh some more kind. I especially enjoyed the "early returns" part.

On a completely different subject, it irritates me when someone says "I have absolutely no idea" to every question about which he has the slightest doubt. In many cases, you have to use the "boxed in by extremes" method to force his hand: "Well, did it happen sometime between the birth of Christ and tomorrow?" or "Could it be somewhere between zero and eight billion?" and then close in on him.

Of course, there's more to it than that. In questions involving memory, you and I know how uncooperative brains can be. In those instances, though, a better response would be "I don't remember," since "I have absolutely no idea" implies "I don't remember, I'm not trying to remember, and there's no chance that I will ever remember."

There are also those situations in which an individual has no useful guess. For instance, just this morning I was inquiring about car insurance and was asked what the purchase price of the car had been. I certainly could have guessed, but the range of prices I had in mind was too wide to really be of use to the agent. She could have guessed as well as I could have.

The phrase "I have absolutely no idea" is often accompanied by a mock-rueful smile and a kind of gleam in the eye. The individual seems aggressively proud of the fact that he is unable to help you in any way.

I suppose I could go on and on, but I have absolutely no idea why I should.

* * *

Date: 11/8/95
From: Reagan
Subject: I hear you, buddy

Yes, I got your very amusing message regarding your calm and measured response to your potential critics. Unfortunately, at that time I was heading into a very unpleasant experience with dental pain that ended up in an emergency visit to the dentist. Being incapable of thinking about anything except the HORRIBLE POUNDING PAIN in my mouth, I forgot to message you back.

:(This is how I felt.

(=< Or maybe more like this.

>:o Or this?

No, there just isn't an icon way to convey real dental pain.

***

Date: 11/8/95
From: Kevin
Subject: is a big crybaby

I wasn't pressing you for an immediate response, but I had a horrible, pounding feeling that I had neglected to push "send" before exiting. I hope you are in a condition of relative comfort today.

***

Date: 11/8/95
From: Reagan
Subject: is much better, thank you.

"Subject is a big crybaby." I love it!

I am much better today. Consumer tip: I have never before been tuned in to the whole pain reliever thing. You hear all this stuff about acetaminophen, ibuprofen, and now that new one Aleve, but I just ignore all that stuff. I still like aspirin basically, and I figure all the others are pretty much alike. But now I have seen a difference. After the Novocain wore off yesterday, I had HORRIBLE POUNDING PAIN in my mouth. I took some acetaminophen, and it didn't touch it. I called the dentist, and he said to take ibuprofen. It took about half an hour to kick in, but the pain was gone, gone, gone!

It was great! The difference? Ibuprofen is an analgesic AND an anti-inflammatory, while acetaminophen has no anti-inflammatory effect.

This is a difference I will not soon forget.

Your manuscript is waiting for me at home. I have prepared my palate by reading a Dean Koontz book full of gratuitous sexual violence. More later.

***

Date: 11/9/95
From: Reagan
Subject: Your big achievement

November 1995: Little Witch 51

Well, you really have written a book. I was up quite late finishing it. It really captured me. I guess the main thing is, it has no feeling of amateurishness at all. When I was reading it, it was just like reading a real book by a real writer. In fact, in a number of passages the writing just completely impressed and moved me. I would say the quality of the writing ranges from "marketable/professional" to at least "very good." I don't recall any passages that clunked, or were hard to follow, or in some other way fell short of the writer's craft.

When I contemplate the really powerful and evocative passages I am intrigued to think what you could produce unfettered by the confines of this genre. The thought is almost intimidating.

Actually I'm already pretty intimidated. I am not sure I will be as much help to you as I had anticipated. You are operating at a level well above my experience. In an attempt to give you some helpful feedback, I am going to try to record my reactions to my initial reading of the book in a memo, and then go back through the book again in an editorial and proofreading mode. I think there might be about a half a dozen typos.

I found the book disturbing and painful. I don't mean this as a criticism at all, quite the contrary. Some of the protagonist's missteps hit pretty close to home. I don't mean that it was a chore to read it. It was intriguing and "a real page turner." It was just so painful to have to "live through" some of what the protagonist experienced.

I have the impression that the last part of the book, beginning with the fire in the apartment, could use some examination. Bear in mind, however, that I think about 90% of the books I read and movies I see have endings that are in the "failure/major disappointment" category, so I may tend to be a bit overcritical in this regard.

I feel that I am not communicating my thoughts and feelings on this very well. I'm really just pretty stunned that you: (1) wrote a book and (2) that it's so good. I'm also a little stunned by the rather remarkable sex scenes, which are, well, really something!

I guess I thought I was going to be able to help you make the text into a marketable book, but there doesn't really seem to be any need for that. There may be some polishing to do, and maybe some fleshing out, but it didn't seem to me that there were problem passages or serious problems with the plot or narrative line that need to be "fixed." I will try to give you feedback that will help you make it even better. But this is all bit over my head: I may only be able to point you in a direction, or make a general suggestion.

Regarding the length issue: I think the STORY only NEEDS just a little more length, and I think I can point to a few areas in that regard. The story is actually complete, or maybe 98% complete, now. However, I think the BOOK could ACCOMMODATE quite a bit more length, and the question then is whether that would improve either the overall quality of the book or its marketability. Again, I think I could point to some areas where subplots or fleshing out COULD be done. For example, I think another scene with Posie (great name!) and the protagonist early in the book would be appropriate and useful. Also, I'll take as much of the "crude guy" as you can write. This could be seen as "padding," but it is at least worth considering.

Anyway, CONGRATULATIONS! More soon.

* * *

Date: 11/10/95
From: Kevin
Subject: is grinning and bearing it

Is it really necessary to "grin" and bear it? Shouldn't one . . . well, I can't think of anywhere to go with this that wouldn't be entirely predictable, so I'll drop it.

Thanx 1,000,000, as they say, for the immensely encouraging note. Deborah asked me recently what I was expecting in the way of criticism from you, and after some thought, I said that very likely you would end up pointing out those areas which I suspected of weakness but was hoping might slip by. This is certainly true of the end, which I think is about as well-written as the rest of the book but is handicapped by a fair amount of triteness, particularly the idea of Karen dying quietly in a flood of sunshine.

I, too, am very fond of Mark, and find myself looking for any opportunity to have him show up as I continue writing. I also think that your idea of having an earlier scene with Posie and Wes is a good one and will very likely do so.

Anyway, back to Mr. Word Processor. Looking forward to further suggestion from you.

* * *

Date: 11/13/95
From: Reagan
Subject: is grimacing and bearing it

As the book has sunk in a bit, it seems to me that Posie is really one of the most interesting characters in it. This is a problem in that she only has one scene, and she is such a complex and surprising character that the scene is almost jarring. One doesn't expect minor characters to just waltz in and be so surprising. (Of course, I suppose that having minor characters who are too authentic is a problem most authors would love to have.) An earlier scene laying a little groundwork for why she behaved that way would be very helpful, as we have discussed. Also, as a reader I wanted a scene with her after Wes returned home, just to see her reaction and maybe get a bit of a happy ending feeling, or maybe a kind of complex and real "as happy an ending as you get in real life but with some lasting consequences" feeling.

Like, I could imagine her loving him and being happy to have him back, but in her precocious way also treating him more as an equal, as if he still had her love and a relationship with her, but had lost his authority as a father over her, so it would be bittersweet, particularly when you look down the road to her adolescence and see that she will really need a father, but will be too knowing and too canny to let him get that authority back over her even though she would benefit from it. "There are some things you just can't undo." Here is a quote from Dr. Jekyll and Mr. Hyde that really struck me recently: "It is one of those affairs that cannot be mended by talking."

Finally, in the one big scene she has now, I thought it might be effective (or would it be trite?) for her, just as she is getting out of the car to walk home, to choke up and start crying just as she says goodbye, with the idea "she almost pulled it off" in terms of the brave detective act she was putting on as a reaction to her father leaving like that.

On another note, I suggested to Mom that she not read the book, but she was going to anyway until Annie talked her out of it later. Annie has some pretty strong (actually very strong) objections to the sex in the book. It bothers me too, but I've become such a reactionary on those issues lately that I'm not sure I trust my own judgement.

It's funny, but the scenes that have really stuck with me in terms of feeling horrified or deeply affected are not the mystic horror ones, but the more prosaic one: Wes being called to Ben's office, Wes packing and leaving home, Wes running into Karen at the mall, etc. I have a feeling that you could go back through this book, take out most of the sex and all of the mysticism, flesh out the characters, and have a real powerful straight novel. Of course, I have no idea what impact that would have on marketability. Actually, since that is a book I would probably like more, it would almost certainly be less marketable.

Is there any way to add maybe two more scenes that flash to the younger sister's life before the one in which she gets a beating? That is a very powerful scene, but it is mystifying, which of course it is supposed to be, but maybe if you could lay the groundwork with a scene in which she has some verbal confrontation with her father and sneaks out of the house, and then one of her doing her dancing thing, and then the one you have now. That would ease into it a bit more.

I feel like I am just being so critical here, which I don't mean to sound like. It's not like I could write anything nearly this good, so why should I throw stones? I'm really just trying to give you all the suggestions I can, and you can take them for what they're worth.

***

Date: 11/13/95
From: Kevin
Subject: is done being clever

Hey, thanks for the comments! I certainly place a great value on your thoughts and ideas. Don't worry about being too critical – rejection and criticism are things I'll have to live with for a long time if I end up staying in the writing biz.

I've already taken your advice to have more of Posie at the beginning. I expanded a couple of her scenes to give the reader a better taste of her personality up front. I really like the "break down at the last minute" idea, and will definitely give it a try. As far as having her show up at the end – it sounds like it's worth trying, and I'm beginning to think about ways I could do that.

The sex scenes: Well, they bother me, too. Is this my version of the casting couch, compromising myself to get a start? Will I look back on this book with great shame? Will it restrict my future as a writer? For the most part, I wrote those scenes first, because they were easy to write and provided some fairly sure-fire punch to the story. My main concern at that point was to write a book that would sell, and to break out of what I feared would be a dry, static writing style. My feeling is that in the second case, it worked. A fairly kinetic story grew up around the sex and the characters came alive outside the bedroom.

I'm getting the feeling that you are right in your observation that the nastiest stuff could be dispensed with at this point and an effective, but less degrading book would result. It's certainly a temptation. My guess is that it would take me a lot longer to sell that book, that I'd be leaving a lot more to luck and to chance than I am with the book in its current format. At this point, as broke and in debt as I am, there is certainly a strong temptation to get paid fast. I'm also concerned that if I tried such major surgery with what little writing skill I've accumulated so far, I would end up with a great expenditure of time and effort and a wrecked book.

Still, I'm not very happy about having a book published that I have to hide under a pen name and advise many of my friends and family not to read. I'm also having a hard time figuring out how, if at all, my work differs from the sort of crap that I've reviled for so long.

Well, enough on that for now. It's good that you've provided me with the impetus to write down how I'm feeling about the whole issue.

As for the sister, I have already added a chapter between her first and second appearances which develops her a little more in a scene with her boyfriend (which does not involve sex).

Thanks much. I look forward to future messages.

* * *

Date: 11/13/95
From: Reagan
Subject: is clever being done

Your last message was intriguing. I guess I can see you doing the sex scenes first would loosen up your writing, although that would never have occurred to me. And it worked: one of the first things I really liked about your writing was the spontaneity, the way stray ideas and concepts were just woven into the narrative, with a real feeling of freshness and creativity. I really enjoy that kind of writing, when you get those "bonus nuggets" of insight into people and life along with the story. I don't mean techno stuff or the product of some kind of other research by the writer, but just stuff, and humor, and little extra twists.

Putting aside the moral issues, I think your sex scenes are well written. They are quite different from the usual, not just in the acts they engage in, but in how it is presented, for example the characters not just being swept away by tides of passion, but more or less calculating their moves and evaluating their partners' responses.

So I don't think the quality of the writing is any problem. The scenes are explicit and offbeat enough that it probably falls into the realm of really well-written pornography, if there is still a line demarking that realm from the realm of literature. For myself, the scenes left me feeling rather turned-off and sullied, but I am perhaps more prudish in this area than many people. I suppose, looking at it from a merchandising perspective, it might be easier for a publisher to ask you to cut some out than to ask you to put more in, so you may be erring on the side of caution. On the other hand, if you have strayed over some unwritten line, then you may get rejected out of hand as being too hardcore. I have no idea how to assess the risks.

I believe there is some tradition of good writers having written actual pornography under pen names in their salad days, so that aspect perhaps should not trouble you so much. To me, the hard thing would be how to handle it with your kids. Do they know you have written a book? You could just publish it under a pen name and simply refuse to reveal it to them until they are in their thirties or something, at which time in might just all seem like a hoot.

More food for thought: Annie says if she found out some parent we knew had written that book she wouldn't let our kids go over to that person's house to play with that person's kids, so you might want to consider keeping this text under wraps until you edit it a bit, or else again just publish it under an assumed name, and when your friends ask you about it, be real mysterious and come up with some impressive sounding pseudo-artistic reason why you won't publish under your own name.

This does all make me want to go to a bookstore and see how this actually compares to the current fare.

I will try to assess this as best I can as I go back through the book more carefully.

As to squaring getting this published with our general condemnation of such fare, I share your plight. I would really love to see you get published and launched on a writing career. Just having written a book is quite an achievement. The fact that it's so good is remarkable. And then if you got it published that would be just an astonishing achievement. To then say "Well that's all well and good, but this book really isn't my cup of tea" seems a bit picky. Perhaps you just need to forge ahead. Maybe the problem will be solved by an editor saying, "We'll be happy to publish it, but you have to tone down the sex." Maybe this is an affair that cannot be mended by talking.

* * *

Date: 11/13/95
From: Kevin
Subject: quit copying me! Mom, he keeps copying . . .

Boy, am I grateful that I have you as a partner in this project! Well, right to it. As to the scenes being written differently, what I tried to do to differentiate them from standard-fare pornography was to have my voice be clinical and descriptive, and leave any coarseness in thought and language to the characters. In other words, the narrative was just concerned with accurately describing the actions of the characters involved, and any vulgarity was what one might expect of those characters under the circumstances. The pornographic effect is the result of the explicitness and the activities which are presented. Which, I guess, adds up to what you described as, "well-written pornography."

As to going over the line with potential publishers, I may come up with a toned-down alternative version to send to publishers and agents expressing an interest in the book, maybe more like an R-rated version. Actually, the idea of a rating for the thing led me to the idea of two published versions of the book, a soft-R and an X version. They could be brought out simultaneously or staggered, kind of like R movies that go to video uncut. That way, I'd have something that most people I know or are related to could read without much offense, and if the kids somehow got hold of it, it wouldn't be as great a shock.

I think Annie is correct in her concern about the impact of the book, as currently composed, on other parents, and I feel bad about causing Annie herself so much distress. I do thank her for providing me with a very illuminating perspective on this book's potential impact on readers, though. That is just what I need as I decide how to proceed.

"Forge ahead" you said. That brings up my thoughts and feelings on why I've been so reluctant to tone down the manuscript. My history of deep-rooted timidity makes me wonder if I'm simply too frightened to proceed with a controversial project. Of course, "controversial" is the universal cover word for all kinds of hideous activity, and I don't want to use that concept to shield myself from valid criticism, but I don't want to shy away from doing something valid and powerful just because I don't want to stick my neck out.

I wonder also if I have somehow set myself up for a major failure here, if there's still some dark remnant of my past turning what was looking like a real-world success into a no-win decision between moral failure and commercial failure.

And you're right, I don't want to get it published as is and then wring my hands as the tortured, reluctant artist afterwards. Whatever I decide to do, I want to feel strongly behind it and act likewise.

* * *

Date: 11/13/95
From: Kevin
Subject . . . me, tell him to stop!

One further thought: your comment about a publisher asking me to tone it down fit in with a thought I had this afternoon that I'm probably limiting my potential audience to a relatively small group of readers. I keep thinking "sex sells," but in modern-day America, it's still mostly titillation and suggestion.

***

Date: 11/14/95
From: Reagan
Subject: He touched me!

Another interesting message. I don't know what is more impressive: that you wrote well or that you thought about how to write well and then did it on purpose. I can see how your approach to the sex scenes produced the result they did, and why they seem different than, for example, sex scenes in romance novels. The writing itself is not passionate. There are aspects of this that perhaps we should discuss over the phone.

Interesting idea to send two versions of the book together to publishers. You could just explain the difference in the cover letter. I think it's a cool idea. I can't really see any downside to it, and it would cover your bases pretty well. They could pick whichever they liked, or even publish both, as you suggest, although that seems somewhat unlikely for a first book. You could call the more hardcore one "The Little Witch Does Dallas" to differentiate it.

I think it would be kind of funny if you did a version in which everything is the same, except that instead of having sex, they would play canasta. Wes could be this real heavy duty canasta freak, by Trish is just not that interested anymore. Then you could give that version to your friends and relatives.

I am making slow progress through the book in the editing/proofreading mode. I may have to send it back to you in chunks, or else ease up and start being a little less detailed.

Regarding forging ahead: I think you owe yourself some selfishness in your life. You have to catch up on doing what is good for your own self. I guess my thought would be to take a hard look at what your best shot at getting published is, and carpe it by the nuts. This book really is just the sort of thing our society doesn't need more of right now, and we both know it, but it's a drop in the ocean at this point, and if you hit the big time, you will have ample opportunities to write caring and healing books. Actually, there seems to be a growing market for caring and healing books right now, including overripe tripe like the Bridges, and semi-mystic stuff like books about angels and Celestine. I think you could probably write really good stuff that would meet what seems to be this growing hunger for goodness, values, and meaning amongst the public. I think of that vignette you did with "Waiting for Her Lover." It was dark, but it pointed up your ability to really write that kind of internal emotional stuff very effectively. And in this book, you seem to be able to evoke the meaning and emotions of real people and real lives in what reads as an effortless and unforced manner.

Anyway, getting back to the point, I guess right now I would say that here is your big chance to pursue the career of your dreams, and you're right, it doesn't really seem like the right time for any timidity or second-guessing. If you can, maybe you should just say: "My only criterion is to put this book into the most marketable form, so I can get a deal. I can always work with the editor on the content, if need be, once the ink is dry on the contract. Once I feel I have a career going, I can refine my craft and the time and the chances to write just exactly the books I want to write."

In the meantime, you certainly do have a lot to be proud of already. First, you seized the steering wheel of your life, and steered it the way you wanted to go, taking big risks in doing so. Then, without really any training or experience, you wrote a book! You pretty much just made up your mind and did it. That isn't supposed to work. Plus, it's well written, which again really isn't supposed to happen that way. If that isn't enough, just tell yourself that the book has moral value as an effective cautionary tale. It actually could convince some number of men not to have an affair. If I had been tempted by an office romance when I read this book, it would certainly have made me think twice!

Regarding pen names: Stephen King first wrote under the name "Bachman." Accordingly, I would suggest you could use "Beethovenman," or perhaps "Stravinskyman."

Hey, what about "Straussman?" That actually sounds pretty good!

***

Date: 11/14/95
From: Reagan
Subject: No short-term memory

Do you ever save or print our e-mail? I've been keeping a partial printed version just for the heck of it, and I've been trying not to be real compulsive about it, but I forget to print about half of mine before I send them (such as the last one) and I sort of regret it.

***

Date: 11/14/95
From: Kevin
Subject: He punched me! Real hard!

I've saved all the sex chapters "as is" and am now mostly done with a first round of surgery. The new scenes are not substantially altered. Mostly, I have substituted more currently acceptable alternatives for the most potentially disturbing parts. The standard I'm using is: if my girls somehow got hold of the book, would I be horrified or just really embarrassed? It actually hasn't been as big a chore as I thought. The next step down, if I decide to take it, would involve much more extensive alterations, but I think it could be done successfully. I don't feel that I need to do it at this point.

I've tried to avoid having to do research for the book, so I think canasta is out. I just don't know anything about it. Try this, though: "The dishwater felt warm and wet as he slowly moved his fingers through it; the fragrant detergent made the long, firm silverware feel slippery in his grasp . . ."

Don't fret about your editing process. You've already given me a great deal of feedback, so don't kill yourself.

Thanks for the further encouragement concerning the beginning and future of my writing career. I know that I've been troubled lately, but overall I'm becoming more excited about being a writer and more enthusiastic about the writing process.

How about "Schumannman"?

Yes, I keep hardcopies of all incoming and outgoing messages, although instead of considering myself "compulsive," I think of myself as being "anally augmented."

Since I had your message in the system, I was able to return it to you without retyping it.

* * *

Date: 11/14/95
From: Reagan
Subject: He threw the dog out the window!

Your re-send worked, more or less. I got a strangely spaced version of the entire text, absent about half of the first paragraph.

Interestingly, your follow-up message contained the following sentence:

"The standard I'm using is: if my girls somehow got hold of the book, would I be horrified or jgent made the long firm, silverware feel slippery in his grasp . . ."

I suspect the message did a little self-editing there.

* * *

Date: 11/14/95
From: Kevin
Subject: He threw the dog out the window!

Okay, here's the missing portion, assuming that you weren't just yanking my chain.

The standard I'm using is: if my girls somehow got hold of the book, would I be horrified or just really embarrassed? It actually hasn't been as big a chore as I thought. The next step down, if I decide to take it, would involve much more extensive alterations, but I think it could be done successfully. I don't feel that I need to do it at this point.

I've tried to avoid having to do research for the book, so I think canasta is out. I just don't know anything about it. Try this, though: "The dishwater felt warm and wet as he slowly moved his fingers through it; the fragrant detergent made the long, firm silverware feel slippery in his grasp . . ."

So there. Ha ha. Mighty funny when it's retyped.

* * *

Date: 11/17/95
From: Kevin
Subject: Why bother? It'll just get chopped off i

Okay, here's the test note that the geniuses at Prodigy told me to send. Hey, did I tell you the one about the silverware? I can never remember when I've told someone a joke. Boy, I can't think of anything to write to just fill up space.

Oh, wait, I was going to send you some speech ideas for your next speech:

1. Compensating workers. Why?

2. Spotting fraudulent claims and tossing their asses in jail.

3. Musical composition: the new therapy for depression.

4. Getting a grant to move from the bureau into a large closet.

5. I'm sorry, sir, but nothing could compensate you for that haircut. Ha ha.

6. I keep saying "Worker's Compilation Bureau." Weird.

7. Workeau Comper's Burensation.

8. Waglo Knudler Gop.

* * *

Date: 11/17/95
From: Reagan
Subject: RE: Why bother? It'll just get chopped off i

I think your message was accurate, although I do have some concern about the last two lines.

Actually, the last two lines were unbelievably funny. Like some kind of randomizing text deconstruction computer program.

I have many thoughts, but no time in which to type them. Sorry. Talk to you this weekend.

* * *

Date: 11/22/95
From: Kevin
Subject: strangeness

I came across one of those medical research ads in the paper, this one for depression, and was intrigued by the peculiar wording of the symptoms checklist. Here it is, exactly as printed.

> I feel downhearted & blue.
> I don't seem to have energy I used to have.
> I have trouble sleeping through the night.
> My concentration is not very sharp.
> I feel tearful & sad.

I'd just rather be by myself.
My appetite isn't very good.
I feel I've let some people down.
I'm pretty indifferent about most things.
My whole body feels rather heavy.

* * *

Date: 11/24/95
From: Reagan
Subject: Heavy body, man.

Having read many psychological records in my current work, the strange language of that ad was not so surprising to me. There is an odd tenor to psychologists' attempts to draft symptoms in plain English. I must say, however, that the list of descriptions you sent seems to hit it pretty well on the head in terms of what depression feels like. I have never really had "clinical" depression problems myself, but some of the hard times I went through not so long ago did depress me in a normal way, and I think I at least have had some vision of what serious depression looks like.* I thought the "heavy body" item was particularly evocative, and would be a good one for separating clinical depression from regular depression. It makes me teary and blue just thinking about it.

Crammed myself with tasty vittles yesterday. I keep thinking there should be more to Thanksgiving. We need to develop some new "traditions." Maybe Thanksgiving music would help. Actually, I understand that "Over the River and Through the Woods" may have originally been associated with Thanksgiving, but I'm not real sure.

Pilgrim Dad and Son:

```
  |
 /|o |
 \|o^|
  |

 <|:|
```

When I look back on these years now, I mostly remember them as a challenging but exciting time that ended with great success and launched my career as a business manager. But at the time, it felt pretty awful. People told me I was crazy to take a job that seemed likely to end in disaster. I felt guilt and uncertainty about uprooting and relocating my family. The stress level in the office was very high; it was not unusual to see people crying at work. We were the target of continual, harsh public criticism and attacks. And, especially during this first year, we had no inkling of the level of success we would achieve; there was no bright light at the end of the tunnel.

4. December 1995: MacGyver, Jr.

Date: 12/7/95
From: Kevin
Subject: "Feelings"

I'm feeling that I need to wrap up the changes to my first draft, so I'm wondering if you could send the manuscript back without worrying that you haven't done enough. You've already contributed plenty to improving the story, so don't sweat it. I really appreciate all of your efforts.

* * *

Date: 12/8/95
From: Kevin
Subject: Latest news

I wrote a short-short story called "My Affair," about a man who falls in love with himself. I sent it to the New Yorker. Fun stuff.

Next up will be further work on "Little Witch." I've let it sit for a while, so I can look at it with some freshness. Basically, I'm just not comfortable with the length, and I need to find out how to expand the book, perhaps with background, depth, and detail, without making it sluggish.

I'm also sketching out an idea for a short, nonfiction book about coping with depression*, concentrating on concrete, practical advice (as opposed to "Come on, you lazy piece of shit! Get your ass in gear!").

I know this sounds odd, but I can't remember now, what, aside from the ADD, you suffered from. I had depression based on a negative self-image, and you had . . . ? Anyway, I know that it would be very helpful to talk to you again about coping strategies while preparing the book. In fact, as I'm writing this, it occurs to me that it could be a collaborative effort. You already have a fair amount of self-help knowledge written down, and it seems to me that much of it could apply to depression as well as to whatever the hell you had.

Now I'm suspicious. What WAS your problem, pal . . . well, here I am, setting up yet another lackluster comedy bit . . . Were you PANTS TOO BIG or something? When I'M feeling blue, I just BORE THROUGH SOLID ROCK with my BARE HANDS until I WORK UP A GOOD SWEAT, and then I . . .

As an adolescent and young adult I had experienced a period of emotional dysfunction, including depression, and I was keen on recording what I had learned from that experience for the benefit of others.

* * *

Date: 12/13/95
From: Kevin
Subject: arfarfarfarfarfarfarfarfarfarfarfarfa

ÿWPC‡

Well, I just tried to import a file from my word processing program and what you see above is what I got. You'll have to take my word for it that the original was much more interesting, although I could provide some excerpts. For instance, "WP" I wrote, in one particularly moving passage. "ÿ" I exclaimed, inviting the reader to share my joy. "C‡" I intoned, suggesting caution.

Okay, I was really trying to send you a copy of the notes/outline that I have for the self-help book. I'll work on it.

* * *

Date: 12/13/95
From: Reagan
Subject: Downer opus

Title for the new book: "Depressed? You Don't Even Know What Real Trouble Looks Like, Buddy!"

"My Affair" sounds fascinating. May I see it?

In answer to your question, I believe I was suffering from "lack of specificity syndrome." It's a particularly difficult disorder to describe, which, by the way, is the disorder's sole diagnostic criterion.*

When I'm feeling blue, I just rush immediately to the mirror, and there I am, not blue at all, but sort of a salmon color, or what used to be called Crayola's "fleshtone" in less enlightened times, and the feeling passes.

Am I capable of saying anything serious in this message? Depends on what you mean by "say." I can't actually speak out loud via internet e-mail. Why the very thought's absurd!

My life is a frenzied whirl. A FRENZIED WHIRL I TELL YOU! Details when I have about ten seconds to actually breathe.**

Wisecracks aside, about a year earlier I had been diagnosed with Attention Deficit Disorder (ADD). This was quite a surprise, because the idea that adults could have ADD was a new one; previously it was assumed to be a childhood condition that people just outgrew. I was actually diagnosed by a pediatrician who was ahead of her time in recognizing that it continued into adulthood. This diagnosis was an important turning point in my life. For some years I took medication that provided significant help while I gradually learned the skills and techniques that allowed me to successfully adapt. Part of what made the year covered by these emails so difficult is that I was early in this process and therefore seeking to meet severe workplace challenges while hindered by ADD.

**For anyone who wasn't there, it's impossible to convey how difficult the situation was at the Bureau. As we dug in, we discovered problem after problem. For example, we were finding many, many claims in which hearings had not been held, sometimes many months after they had been requested. Every day, we were printing copies of claim files and shipping boxes of them to the law firms we had hired to help us get caught up. Many of these claims were from people with serious injuries who urgently needed our help.*

***

Date: 12/15/95
From: Kevin
Subject: I'm far too frenzied to enter a subject

I like the title suggestion. My new idea: "I Was So Depressed I Couldn't Even DRIVE to a Bookstore, You Faker!"

I just tried to "import" the short story, and a Helpful Hints box popped up wondering if I wouldn't rather "attach" it instead. So, I will attempt to do so. Let me know if you get it.

I think I see a tremendous thesis opportunity in your condition: ". . . and since the subject was, in the end, forced to admit to at least one recurrence of what was, in the Thomas-Kincaid study, shown to be a technical (if not practical) symptom, he was immediately dismissed from the test group, leaving a total of . . ."

It would be fun to come up with a set of 50s-early 60s crayon colors: Bleached Blonde, Lipstick, Bourbon, Lush Lawn . . .

Don't worry, if I want you to say something serious, I'll TELL you to say something serious you maggot! You eyeballin' me, boy? I say, are you EYEBALLIN' me? You BETTER not be . . .

Okay, I just tried to Send, and was told by Mr. Helpful Hints that "attachments cannot be sent to Internet recipients." So, all you're getting is this note. Hope you've enjoyed it.

***

Date: 12/15/95
From: Kevin
Subject: Okay, I lied. I'm not frenzied.

So, I was shopping for a Christmas present for you and ended up with the following guidelines:

1. Inexpensive (I'm trying to be a semi-responsible adult and not burst into flaming debt)

2. Easy to use (you're too busy to put together a model, read a book, or wipe your ass more than twice)

3. Something you can do with the kids (combining a fun activity for you with quality family time, for optimal time usage)

4. Comes in a box (easy to wrap)

5. Doesn't smell like old fish (so you won't be offended by the stench)

6. Soothes the frenzied heart (may reduce medical insurance premiums. Check with your health care professional for details.)

7. Has the right balance of carpe and diem (self-explanatory)

8. Fleshtone (in a positive, inclusive sort of way)

9. Tastes like chicken (but only half the fat!)

10. Won't put its cold, clammy hands around your throat in the middle of the night ('nuff said!)

Hope you enjoy it!

***

Date: 12/15/95
From: Kevin
Subject: FW: English?

Quote of the Week (mother speaking to her seven-year-old daughter in McDonald's):

"You're gonna finish your fuckin' food! I ain't shittin'!"

* * *

Date: 12/15/95
From: Reagan
Subject: Re: Okay, I lied. I'm not frenzied.

Really makes you cringe, doesn't it? There's nothing that depresses me more than to see some little child out at a restaurant or a mall with obviously defective parents. All that potential for love, happiness, and growth in that child, and you can just see the road of unhappiness, coarsening, and disillusionment coming. I'm not kidding, I get real teary. I volunteered to serve meals at a homeless shelter once and I could never do it again. Those kids would come by, little four-year-olds, and they didn't really know yet that they were living miserable outcast lives, but you could just see that day coming, maybe a few days into first grade, when the rejection would kick in, and they'd be going down a dark road. Taking shot after shot to their self-esteem until the damage is irreversible.

I just can't handle seeing children harmed, even in movies. I just try to block it out. That's chickenshit, I know, but that's a real hardwired emotional button for me.

On a lighter note, we can all be grateful that the mother was, in fact, not shitting in McDonald's.

* * *

Date: 12/20/95
From: Kevin
Subject: Nights of the living dead

I'm just now getting to my mail for the first time in many days. I fell ill Saturday night and only now feeling glimmerings of wellness. This is like those Godawful cases of the flu that we got as kids, except that this one came with three full days of bad muscle pains. But hey, a least I'm not shitting in McDonald's.

I didn't mean to shoot you off into such a dismal tangent with my last note, but you're right, it can get to you pretty easily if you let it. I don't think you should be calling yourself "chickenshit," though. It's possible to be too sensitive, and to care too much, but that's no crime.

* * *

Date: 12/20/95
From: Reagan
Subject: Was roses.

Judging by what I actually bought for you, here are the criteria my subconscious must have been following:

1. Looks a lot cheaper than it really is.

2. Small size and generally unimpressive appearance.

3. Requires batteries, which I may have forgotten to buy and enclose.

4. No immediate "wow" impact, gift only appreciated many months later, after recipient forgets who even gave it to him.

5. Completely puzzles recipient's new spouse, makes her question gift-giver's judgement.

6. Odd-shaped packaging, impossible to wrap attractively.

7. Could be useful to a proctologist.

8. I wanted one, so I bought one for you.

Actually, criterion number 8 is the only one I ever really apply, and if it leads to some quirky gift choices, I guess that's just part of the price of being related to me.

I'm glad I won't be strangled at night by cold clammy hands, or, if I am, that I will at least know it won't be your fault.

Reagan D chose your gift to him to open as his early present, and it was a BIG HIT! We have already made the "irritating siren" and the "invisible power radio." With all the little troubles in his life, it is just such a huge pleasure to see him just going right at this kind of creative stuff. His inventiveness and tenacity are awesome. I was sick the other night, and the females were gone. Left to himself, he didn't watch TV or anything like that, he just created stuff. Like he spent about an hour attaching a flashlight to his big model train as a headlight (which was trickier than it sounds) and running it around the track in the dark. Anyway, the circuit set is great, as he can follow the maps and make the stuff on his own, and he really will go through and make them all.

Now is my season of retrospection and contemplation. Who am I, and what do I want to do? The euphoria of having sidestepped disaster* has faded, and I find myself filling with, simultaneously, contentment and unease. More later.

Apologies time 1,000,000 for not mailing the transcript. No excuse, SIR!

**I'm not sure which narrowly avoided disaster I was referring to here. There were many. We were working hard to fix the company but in these early years it seemed like every triumph would be followed by three new crises.*

* * *

Date: 12/21/95
From: Kevin
Subject: Was what? Roses? Rosebud?

Man, if your gift to me really lives down to its billing, I'll be very impressed! I can hardly wait! Oddly enough, when I was shopping for Reagan D's present, I had to choose between the circuit set and the Dr. Procto children's starter set. I figured he'd love it, but the rest of you might get tired of "covering your asses." Nyuk nyuk.

I'm really glad to hear that he has continued in his inventive and curious ways. He sure is a dynamo inside, and I hope he can find some way of at least peacefully coexisting with the world while he finds a good outlet for his talents.

Perhaps you have Seasonal Retrospection Thingy.

*** * * * ***

Date: 12/21/95
From: Reagan
Subject: was a pop cultural reference

"The Subject Was Roses" was a play, or book, or movie, or something. Why I decided to refer to something I obviously know nothing about is a mystery. Just part of my charm, I guess.

If you gave Reagan D a Dr. Procto Jr. set, I really would have to watch my ass. When you give something like that to Reagan, he really uses it. Last night, he made the "burglar alarm," which is standard. Then he taped the little earphone to the microphone of his tape player, so the alarm would be generally audible through the player's speaker. Then he strung a trip wire across the living room and laid in wait with his Nerf bow and arrow, attacking "intruders" who tripped the alarm.

This morning, before he ate breakfast, he made a telegraph for show and tell.

Gratifying, isn't it?

*** * * * ***

Date: 12/22/95
From: Reagan
Subject: is behind the curve

Menny Hoopnidays!

Has our box of presents for you arrived yet? If it hasn't, there isn't one darn thing I can do about it.

I still haven't bought a computer! At least my decision will be easier at this point: I'll just go out and buy whatever pathetic system is still available for sale in Bismarck. Soon, I hope, I will be e-mailing you from home, and will have a new address to give you. Also, I suspect Monica will want to do some e-mailing with the cousins.

Hapno Christledings!

* * *

Date: 12/22/95
From: Kevin
Subject: Mellow Huladays

That boy is going to be launching himself to the Moon before you know it, in a ship made out of a refrigerator box and powered by frog excrement. He's MacGyver, Jr.

I have reason to believe that the box is in Omaha, due to a yellow slip left by the Post Office. I will be retrieving it today. UPS has the better way, "hiding" the boxes, often by leaving them right next to the front door, with a little post-it note on the door saying "We left some boxes next to your door. Hope you are the intended recipient and not a thief. Thank you."

Maybe what you should do is get really funky and find an old punch-card system – no monitor, no modem, no nothing. I'll get one too, and we'll send each other packets of cards. Retro, dude.*

I've been worried that Sabrina will be disappointed with her Christmas gift. It revolves around the Pink Ranger, and you indicated that Reag has been sad to see the Power Rangers abandoned by everyone else. I had been pleased to see Sabrina at least somewhat interested in what was mostly a boy phenomenon, and when I saw this particular toy, I just grabbed it. Oh, well, as you said, there's nothing I can do about it now.

Havno Christledings . . . try the shop around the corner . . . Moe always has plenty of Christledings.

I took what I recall being the first computer class offered by my high school in Minot, North Dakota, in 1975. We "programmed" stacks of punch cards and then took them to the college to run. I don't recall it ever working.

* * *

Date: 12/29/95
From: Reagan
Subject: A thought to carpe the diem by

Advantage is gained in war and also in . . . other things by selecting from many or unpleasant alternatives the dominating point. American military thought had coined the expression "Over-all Strategic Objective." When our officers first heard this, they laughed, but later on its wisdom became apparent and accepted. Evidently this should be the rule, and other great business be set in subordinate relationship to it. Failure to adhere to this simple principle produces confusion and futility to action, and nearly always makes things much worse later on.

Winston Churchill
The Gathering Storm

5. January 1996: Spontaneous Long Impassioned Message

Date: 1/2/96
From: Kevin
Subject: Mr. Slow Learner

Just now checked my mailbox. Thanks for the note. Churchill certainly is an inspirational character. The quote you sent says exactly what I'm getting back to just now – the central position that writing must take in my life if I'm to succeed at it. I got thrown off by a few things, particularly that bout with the flu, and am finally getting reconnected with words.

I find myself attracted to stuff like Tank Girl, and Hunter Thompson, and Curly of the Stooges – weirdness, anarchy – that's the direction I need to stretch in, since I've lived so long at the other end of the spectrum. I'll probably never be able to live that kind of life, nor do I really want to (I just don't seem to have the wiring or the constitution for it) but I want to be able to visit, and to write down what I see.

* * *

Date: 1/4/95
From: Kevin
Subject: Warning: Lame Comedy Bit

I thought that, in order to be more Churchillian, I should begin writing quotable stuff:

1. No, that's okay, you just stepped on my foot. No big deal. Really, I'm fine.

2. Dogs are everywhere. Sometimes they seem to be mighty ferocious. Sometimes they're okay and you can pet them. Those are the best kind of dogs.

3. How big is big? In order to comprehend big, one must first fully understand the nature of one's own size relationship to itself – a spatial orientation of primary magnitude. This can be accomplished by, well, I don't know, thinking about it a lot or something.

4. War is a brutal business, my lad.

5. Dieting is like a vacuum cleaner – it sucks, and it sounds like a loud, whirring, whining sort of thing.

6. Tra-la-la-la-la, life is just a bowl of tasty cherries, tra-la-la-la-la.

* * *

Date: 1/4/95
From: Kevin
Subject: Anthems

I've played with the idea of what qualifies as a "rock anthem" since that weak collection was advertised on TV some time ago. To me, it would have to be something big and energetic, something that would make you jump out of your seat if you heard it starting up at a concert. The first one that came to mind was "School's Out." Others that I've thought of since then are "Saturday Night's Alright," "Satisfaction," "Woman from Tokyo," "We will Rock You/We are the Champions," "Revolution" and "Rock and Roll." Most of Def Leppard's hits seem to have an anthemic quality. I've excluded anything by AC/DC on the grounds that I can't stand them. "Smoke on the Water" seems like it should be one, but it's kind of ponderous. Anyway, it's fun to think about while driving. I'm sure you'll have few to add.

* * *

Date: 1/6/96
From: Reagan
Subject: Anthems back at you, man

"School's Out" is also the first anthem I thought of, before I even saw it on your list. Therefore, it must be the standard against which others are judged.

Regarding criteria, I agree that it must be "big and energetic." That's why "Stairway to Heaven" is, at least arguably, not an anthem. The slow, quiet part lasts too long. Let's clarify "big." It has to have a sort of majestic sound. It can't be fast and thrashy. To be completely circular, it has to sound anthemic.

I would add that I think it has to take some sort of position, however misguided. It has to give the listener a feeling of inclusion or group identity. I believe "Satisfaction" does that by establishing a cultural and generational worldview that sets the listener apart from those who are being criticized in the song. I believe "We Will Rock You/We Are the Champions" and "Revolution" also pass muster. I can't recall "Woman from Tokyo." "Saturday Night's Alright" is borderline, as it is a little low on majesty and a little too individualistic, but I can see that it might be an anthem for some people I don't want to have too much contact with. I agree that "Smoke On the Water" is not an anthem. Ubiquitousness is helpful, but not sufficient. It is a narrative, not a statement.

The Monkees theme has anthemic lyrics but lacks the anthemic sound. I would add "For Those About to Rock," although I agree with your position on AC/DC. All of Def Leppard's hits should be categorically excluded on the grounds that they are all artificial attempts to be anthems. How about "My Generation?" Other candidates:

"I Love Rock and Roll" (Joan Jett)

"Give Me That Old Time Rock and Roll (a song I loathe)

"Saturday Night" (Bay City Rollers)

"Another Brick in the Wall" (Pink Floyd, and another song I loathe)

"Cadillac Ranch" (Springsteen, and this one really gives you the anthem feeling, although it doesn't quite have the anthem sound)

As you say, I'm sure there are others. I'm surprised at how few of them I really like. Maybe it's because there are so few rock anthems for wholesome middle-class people from Middle America. Perhaps "Artists Only" by Talking Heads, which, of course, sounds nothing like an anthem at all, and contains the immortal lyrics "you can't see it 'til it's finished." Almost by definition, any anthem that I could relate to would have to be anti-anthemic. I am uncomfortable with tying any of my self-identity to a larger group identity, or with being swept away by mass emotional or non-rational appeals.

I suppose John "Cougar" Mellencamp's "Small Town" comes pretty close to a Middle America rock anthem, but it's still not an anthem for me. Of course, one can enjoy a rock anthem even though one does not really come within the anthem's group, as I enjoy "Satisfaction" or "I Love Rock and Roll," but I would think it would be even more satisfying to have one aimed right at you, and those like you. Perhaps, however, I should find it reassuring that I am not in a cultural cohort that is the target of rock anthems.

Could that have possibly sounded any more arrogant and elitist?

I thought your "Lame Comedy Bit" was extraordinarily funny. I particularly enjoyed "War is a brutal business, my lad." There, it actually made me laugh out loud again when I typed it. The "bowl of tasty cherries" one was also inspired. It was the "tasty" that really got me.

SPONTANEOUS LONG IMPASSIONED MESSAGE ALERT!!!

I was surprised by your "Mr. Slow Learner" message. I had thought you were going in the direct opposite direction, probably because that is what I am doing, and I always tend to assume that you are thinking roughly the same thing I am, because I guess, really, we often are thinking the same thing at the same time.

Anyway, I have really been moving away from what seems to me at this time to be an affectation of strangeness, a la Hunter Thompson or Tank Girl. I mean, I can enjoy that stuff, but it doesn't appeal to me much, in that it seems superficial and meaningless. During adolescence, there is this special powerful attraction to the outre, the offbeat, the rebellious. That attraction always continues somewhat throughout life to some extent, but it doesn't seem like a fruitful road to me right now. It's style, and I'm after substance. Those people have just found a different way of distracting themselves from living life on real terms. Their means are different, but the goal and the result is the same as yuppies pursuing their exercises and BMWs, and addicts using their substances, and zealots using their religions, and most people following their prosaic path of consumerism and non-participatory entertainment.

I don't think being weird is any more meritorious or interesting than being regular. Just the word "weirdness" completely turns me off. It evokes the smug incomprehension of adolescence. "Like, weirdness, man." Also, anarchism strikes me as an ultimate intellectual cop-out, a pseudo-philosophical posture that can be formally defended, and can prove a handy basis for smugness, but that is simply not genuinely valid or fruitful. I don't think you have lived at the other end of the spectrum from weirdness or living on the fringe. If anything, I think you have been tied too much to an attraction to this zeitgeist.

I am convinced that what I need (and so I validly of invalidly assume you need) is to move far away from all such silliness and try to get at the reality of life. Where can one find the reality of life? What pursuits are more than a fruitless distraction? I'm not saying it is not valid to have fun, actually I think I am having more real fun now than I ever had before, and will have more and more fun the more I connect with what's real. The appearance of fun, or the appearance of recklessness and strangeness and abandon, may be real fun for some people, maybe most people, maybe for you too, but not for me. Real fun for me comes when I live life fully, when I am carpeing my diems.

Also, it seems to me that your path to being a really good writer, maybe a great writer, is not at all in that direction. Your writing technique is excellent. Presumably you will get even better technique as you continue to write. But the biggest area where your writing can improve and perhaps needs to improve is simply in your becoming a more fully formed human, just as my legal technique is excellent, but as I become more healthy and more fully formed as a person and as a man my legal work improves, as all aspects of my life improve. I think you and I for years were as strange and weird, or stranger and weirder, than most people would ever care to be, and our path of improvement and progress lead directly away from strangeness and weirdness.

Does this mean we need to become "normal?" Yes and no. We don't need to become prosaic or dull or conventional, but we do need to become healthier and less strange, and perhaps try to become what normal humans SHOULD be: fully realized and authentic. We both seemed quite normal, and live apparently normal live, but we were never even close to actually being normal.

I think the over-riding area in your book that needs re-looking is that you perhaps do not fully grasp yet what "normal" really looks and feels like, from the inside. You present seriously dysfunctional characters with gaping holes in their personalities as being normal. They are interesting, but they are bizarre and deeply flawed. I think the more grounded you become in normalcy and the more you become a fully formed functioning person the better perspective you will have to present such characters in a way that will allow the reader to understand how they became what they are and what impact their strangeness will have on their lives.

I am in this same position. I have been lucky enough to have, through many long discussions with Annie over the years, to have received a sort of ongoing tutorial on normalness from somebody who is both pretty normal and pretty insightful. But I am still just really beginning the process of becoming normal. I feel that once I have myself well grounded, the full possibilities of life will blossom and open to me. That is what will make my life richer and more interesting and more authentic.

January 1996: Spontaneous Long Impassioned Message

What will not work is to go and adopt or try on various lifestyles. I could take up a fitness lifestyle, or a pursuit of money lifestyle, or a lifestyle seeking interesting experiences, or a lifestyle of weirdness, but none of that would get me anywhere real. I believe that introspection is a key part of the real and useful process, as is the casting aside of false distractions and hollow values.

How about this quote I recently read: "To focus on technique is like cramming your way through school. You sometimes get by, perhaps even get good grades, but if you don't pay the price day in and day out, you never achieve true mastery of the subjects you study or develop an educated mind."

It seems to me that weirdness and anarchy are techniques of living. They are a lifestyle choice. They have no value. They are only distractions. Now if you or I look within ourselves and get in touch with what is real in ourselves and in life we will end up making choices of how we live our lives that will be authentic choices for us, and maybe those choices will appear weird to others, but we will not be doing them BECAUSE they are weird.

I think the difference is absolutely crucial. I think this is all absolutely difficult to do. I am still almost completely stuck on the technique level. I am still trying to get to bed on time, and use my calendar regularly, and get the kids involved in activities, and be productive worker, and eat better, and exercise more, and have more fun, and I'm doing pretty well and my life's better than it was but really it's all almost NOTHING. It's not making me who I need to be. When I do the real internal work of becoming Reagan, everything will flow much more naturally. My kids will get so much more from me. Annie will get so much more from me. My life will be so much more interesting and fun and successful. I know this because I've touched and sustained it for brief times.

Am I just completely overreacting here? I realize that your message was just a comment and all, but I guess it just really sparked this sudden outpouring from me and really crystallized my thinking on this stuff. I hope there is something here that is useful to you and I hope it isn't offensive or anything.

***

Date: 1/7/96
From: Kevin
Subject: ?

I'm writing this in response to your massive message. I, too, considered and dismissed "Stairway" for similar reasons.

I haven't really thought about content – it's mostly the sound that I'm after – but content might be useful in narrowing the field down to an album's worth of songs. I can see how, applying your standards, Def Leppard's stuff would be excluded, but I still think they have pretty strong anthemic qualities.

"My Generation" – I thought about this one, and maybe it should be included, but I just don't have much enthusiasm for The Who. It certainly wouldn't be out of place, though.

Your list:

"I Love Rock and Roll" seems more like a song about anthems than one itself

"Old Time Rock and Roll" – I can't stand it either, and it doesn't sound like an anthem to me

"Saturday Night" – Maybe there should be a separate category for Pop Anthems. It does have the right sound.

"Another Brick in the Wall" – Would it make you jump out of your seat cheering at a concert? I'd be yelling "I'm leaving! You suck!"

"Cadillac Ranch" – I don't think so. What about "Born to Run"? Interesting thoughts about group identity. They certainly parallel the idea of national anthems – helping to create and strengthen a national identity.

January 1996: Spontaneous Long Impassioned Message

Your Long Impassioned Message, offensive? No, not any more than if you'd sent it in a box of shit with a small explosive charge in it. Ha! No, just kidding — just being "weird," man. Can't you see how cool it is to be weird? C'mon, be weird with me, man. It's embarrassing with just me. They just stare at me and say, like, "He's weird. Let's leave and never come back." I hate that, man.

But here's the deal: what I'm trying to accomplish is not that kind of weirdness. One thing I'm trying to do is avoid settling myself into well-worn wagon tracks. I want to end up creating at as deep a level as I am capable — writing as much as possible without regard to established conventions of genre and style and the other elements. Well, I shouldn't say "without regard." What I mean is I want to be aware of my options and make decisions about what I'm doing, leaving myself as much leeway as possible.

I also need to fight me natural tendency to either accept things as they are or to work for change in a much too limited manner. I find myself tending to accept situations as permanent and unchangeable, or changeable only within narrow limits. If I'd been running the Graphics Department at Lancer, they'd still be doing manual paste-up on light tables instead of using Mac workstations.

So, what I've been doing is trying to "shake up" my mind, break it open and allow it to think all kinds of thoughts, to travel beyond the old boundaries. I'm still strongly drawn to a state of stillness and repose, and that just won't do. I know that that's the aim of a lot of people, but I've got it nailed. I can be at rest with the best of them. Now I need to get stirred up inside, jumpy and excited. I'm not looking for affectation in my life, I'm looking for a truly altered state of consciousness. I'm just using this stuff as one way of getting there.

I guess I am moving in a somewhat different direction than you right now. I think it's possible that I could change in ways that would make me less effective as a father, husband, and friend, that I might not be as effective in dealing with everyday life. I'm not trying for that result, and I hope it won't happen, but I'm focusing on internal changes that will allow me to be more creative, and how that will affect other aspects of my life I don't know.

I agree with the necessity for real work – and really working, consistently, has been another struggle for me, but I fear that if I try to make myself simply a nine-to-five it's-my-job sort of writer, I'll end up producing polished crap. I feel the need to work internally as well as externally to create at my highest level.

I know what you mean about being stuck at the technique level. I've tried being all sorts of people, but I was working from the skin in. I'm going to hammer on the inside and see what sort of me emerges.

Thanks for all the thoughts. As usual, you are a great catalyst for my own thinking.

* * *

Date: 1/8/96
From: Kevin
Subject: More stuff

I wasn't satisfied with my last message to you, even as I was writing it, and it's because what I was describing is so interconnected with the rest of my life that it doesn't make complete sense taken out of that context. I'm either going to have to make this a very long message, or call you, and with my current time constraints, I think I'll use the phone.

Pop anthem: "Waterloo"?

* * *

Date: 1/10/96
From: Kevin
Subject: Lots of stuff

January 1996: Spontaneous Long Impassioned Message

WARNING: Potential for negative emotions in this section

I've been helping Peggy and Carl move into their new house for the past few days, and mouse droppings were discovered in the garage and in the basement. An exterminator came out and put down traps. I'm not sure what kind he used in the garage, although I think they had some kind of poison. The ones in the basement were just shallow rectangular dishes full of a very sticky substance.

This morning, I was at the house to let workmen in to finish up a few things, and while I was in the basement I heard intermittent squeaking from a pile of boxes. I moved some of the boxes and continued to listen, and eventually found a small, grey mouse stuck fast in one of the traps. It was in the stuff literally from head to toe, with its mouth stuck and its nose barely free to breathe. My immediate reaction was a desire to free it and let it go.

I took it to a sink and began to try pulling it out of the goo, but had a hard time. The substance was certainly well formulated for its purpose. I got the mouse's tail and hind legs free, thinking that if I worked from back to front I would keep it from trying to bite at me in panic. It continued to struggle, not surprisingly, and I had to work to keep free the parts I had unstuck. As I worked on its body, the combination of my efforts and its movements caused it to roll its head down into the sticky stuff, covering one eye and its nose, I tried getting its head up and out, but only injured it in trying to do so.

I could see that it was really suffering, having difficulty breathing, and that the cause was hopeless. I had to kill it, and I wanted to do it as quickly as I could to save it from further pain. Remembering that there was a hand ax in another room (we'd been using the blunt end as a hammer) I ran to get it and brought it back. I held the blade a few inches over the mouse's neck, and tried to force myself to act. The little creature was obviously suffering and I really needed to end its life, but it felt like there was a force pushing up against my arms. I had a glimpse of a scene in "Full Metal Jacket," where one of the soldiers kills the wounded Viet Cong sniper.

I chopped down, and missed. The blade landed in front of the mouse's head. But now that I'd acted, I quickly lifted the ax and chopped again, right on the neck. I hoped that I'd killed it with the one blow – blood began to pour out from the neck – but its legs continued to twitch. I supposed that it was just muscle spasms, but I landed another blow just to make sure.

I was overcome with grief, and lurched off into another room, where I crouched on the floor, crying and trembling. Thoughts began tumbling through my head. Through the grief came a somewhat removed sensation of experiencing the grief. That must be an habitual part of me now – stepping back and observing what I am experiencing or feeling instead of withdrawing or trying to stifle the feeling as I used to do. I also had this thought: "There must be hope for me if what just happened is having this effect on me." I do sometimes fear for my fundamental humanity, despite living a pretty decent life on most levels, but I must say I felt very human at that moment.

These thoughts were quickly followed by suspicion: was I reveling too much in my grief? Was I feeling so proud of my sadness that I was really cancelling it out? I didn't think so, and I still don't. I really felt for that mouse, and I really wanted to save it, and I genuinely felt terrible that I had to kill it.

I cleaned up the area and the axe, wrapped the trap and mouse in Kleenex and then in a plastic bag, and put it in a construction trash bin.

ALL CLEAR: Back to less depressing topics

I got the Tank Girl soundtrack, some of which I like. I looked around to see what I could find in the way of the original comic, and found that the movie was based on an English comic strip (or, rather, a series of multi-page stories appearing in a larger magazine). At a comic store, I was shown a four-part adaptation of the movie, a comic book which was not by the original artist and writer, and a magazine which was the second anthology of the original stories by the creators of the strip. That's what I bought, and boy, was I disappointed. It was crap. It was no better than a mediocre underground comic from the Sixties. Either the quality took a huge dive after the initial stories, or it was never any good to begin with and the movie just made the comic look promising. Oh, well.

* * *

Date: 1/10/96
From: Reagan
Subject: Forgot to drink his coffee, is logy

What a horrible design for a mouse trap. I'll bet the world is not beating a path to that inventor's door. Sure, it kills mice, but doesn't the maker need to factor in the removal and disposal aspects of the mouse extermination process. Maybe it is all part of a subtle plot to dehumanize the population.

I can see how it would be reassuring for you, or for me, to have that emotional reaction. It is nice once in a while to get the message "you are not a sociopath." I have been getting some indications lately that I may be a genuinely nice, or at least pleasant, person, and I find that reassuring in the same way, although less traumatically.

What a disappointment about the Tank Girl comic! The snippets in the movie really did look quite promising, and I had it in the back of my head to read some in the future. Next time I visit I will have to read the anthology to bring closure to my disillusionment process.

Your last message was interesting, or tantalizing. I must admit, I have not understood the decisions you have made in the last 13 months, and your goals and motivations are a mystery to me. I have the sense that you are off on an internal trip that I am not privy to, and I am just hoping it works out well.

Your point about avoiding conservative thinking or assumptions struck a chord with me. Despite the dramatic decisions and changes I have made lately, on reflection I still perceive in myself the inclination or disposition to create and follow a fairly narrow path. It would be good, as you indicated, to somehow inculcate in myself a habit of questioning and innovating, for not just choosing among the options that readily present themselves, but to instead reserve the ability and inclination to look for marked departures and innovations.

* * *

Date: 1/10/96
From: Reagan
Subject: Is now suitably wired with bean juice

> It is not given to human beings, happily for them, for otherwise life would be intolerable, to foresee or to predict to any large extent the unfolding course of events.
>
> Winston Churchill

This is a point of view that I had not really ever considered, but as I consider it, I come to believe that it is a blessing, not a curse, that we cannot see what the future holds for us. It gives us freedom to choose and to act, and from suffering in anticipation of adverse events yet to occur.

* * *

Date: 1/11/96
From: Kevin
Subject: Has also drunk of the nectar of the bean

"Sociopath." That's a good word, but I wonder if it's the right one for me (or us). I just looked it up (in the American Heritage Dictionary) and found this definition: "One who is affected with a personality disorder marked by aggressive, antisocial behavior." When I worry about myself, it's more about a kind of detachment or calculation. However, this sounds odd even as I write it, since I also have the tendency to be sympathetic and empathetic to an uncomfortable degree.

Putting that last thought aside, I have found that as I've gained insights into myself and into others, as I've discovered themes and variations in human nature, it's been hard to avoid the self-suspicion that I'm being calculating and manipulative in my dealings with others. It's possible that in time this feeling will pass. In the meantime, I just have to make sure that my motives in my dealings with others are good ones.

I'm listening to the B-52's first album:

> Everybody goes to parties
> They dance this mess around
> They do the Shu-ga-loo
> They do the Shy Tuna
> They do the Camel Walk
> They do the Hip-o-crit

"Shy Tuna" – I love it.

The past 13 months? Here's a quick version. I'd enjoyed my single time and learned good things from it, but I had tremendous needs for emotional and physical intimacy (touch in all forms, not just sex), and I also needed to experience a positive, long-term, growing relationship with a woman. I found all of that with Deborah, and I'm very thankful that she came along, because I'm sure I would have ended up marrying someone less well-suited to me.

I know you wondered: Why the need to marry? Well, at this stage of my growth, it feels like the only way to be as intimate with another human as I want to be. It's also much easier to explore the nuances of each other within the support of a committed relationship. And marriage provides a strength to a relationship that's hard to come by otherwise. Most importantly, in my case, it felt very much like the right thing to do, and still does. I can't imagine a much better environment in which to grow and work.

I can see how it might appear that I weakened, or took a giant step backwards, but I don't think that this is the case. I suppose a footloose, bohemian lifestyle would seem like a more suitable one for a writer, but for me, at this time, it would siphon off energy and creativity that is better focused on my work.

Being married to someone as comforting and kind as Deborah has given me a tremendous, solid base from which to explore my inner and outer worlds. Maybe I haven't related my explorations as well as I should. I'm trying to take chances intellectually, emotionally, and spiritually, purposely putting myself at risk, using what I learned about strength and survival during all those years of sickness to carry me through. I don't want to sigh, sit back, and think: "Well, I made it through Hell. Now I can take it easy." I want to tear at myself and see if what comes off is just straps and restraints.

I don't want it to sound entirely self-abusive, though. Part of the process is something like the Biblical passage about scales dropping from me eyes – working to see things and people with new understanding, from a different perspective. Too much of my life is a conditioned reflex, which makes living easier, but also duller.

I'm not opposed to the idea of serenity, but the kind I'm after now comes from the getting of knowledge and wisdom, not from my old habits of withdrawal from the world and contracting my needs until they match my circumstances.

New snippet from the book (Wes and Tricia):

> "Oh," she said, smiling warmly as she reached out to touch his cheek. "I've always loved this face. I think you're very handsome." (Is she being straight with me, or is she just in a good mood? Can't tell.)

"Well, thank you, ma'am for that comforting impression of sincerity. My ego thanks you, and my id wants to know if you're wearing any underwear." Tricia let go with an open laugh of real amusement.

I hope you continue to appreciate how much you mean to me. You give my life dimension, security, and love, in quantities that most people never experience. You're someone I can always rely on, for advice, criticism, comfort, and inspiration. I get a lot more out of my experiences because I have you to share them with. Plus, you're funny. Thanks for being you.

I got a call earlier this week from an agent in California. I had submitted a book proposal – one of dozens I've sent out – and she's the first to contact me with a positive response. She wants to see the whole book! And, when I told her that I was working on a depression self-help book, she asked me to write up a book proposal and send it along also. Cool! Progress!

* * *

Date: 1/11/96
From: Kevin
Subject: P.S.

Concerning the quote you sent. Just today, I thought to myself that I enjoyed the idea of wonders to come in my life. It's like Life is going to give me presents occasionally, out of the blue. What a nice feeling.

The quote has a good point, in that foreknowledge can be burdensome. When I see the girls making what I consider to be bad decisions, and know that they'll just have to suffer the consequences in order to learn, it's unpleasant.

Still, it seems pretty fundamentally human to want to see into the future. I know I'll keep trying.

* * *

Date: 1/11/96
From: Reagan
Subject: doesn't know when to shut up

I have had the nagging feeling for years that I have been using the word "sociopath" wrong, and now you have confirmed it. Many years, ago, I read a definition of the word that was basically a person who does not feel that society's rules apply to him, who is unconstrained by moral or even legal rules. I actually think that is a useful definition, and there should be some word that actually carries that meaning. I wonder if it is, actually, an older or truer definition of sociopath. Anyway, whether it's just because most people who feel unconstrained do act aggressively or antisocially and therefore the word took on that connotation, or maybe it's because the definition I read years ago was just plain wrong and too broad, it has become apparent to me that what I have been meaning by sociopath all these years differs from how most people use it. So now I'm going to stop.

"Amoral" comes close, but doesn't quite do it. "Emotionless" is off base.

Anyway, what I was trying to convey was that sense that we were only pretending to have "normal" feelings and behaviors, that we did feel detached in a broad and fundamental way from the norms of our culture. It's odd, because we both behaved in unusually moral ways, most of the time, probably were better behaved than most people, and on some level I have always had a very strong sense of morality, but also on some level a profound disconnection and feeling of detachment.

I used to think, as I suspect many people do, that being capable of amoral behavior gives one power, an edge, an "unfair advantage," a freedom to act without the constraints that restrict most other people, but I was wrong. It is actually part of a crippling package. What I now know is that the stronger my moral base, the more clearly I determine and understand what is right and wrong, what is important and trivial, and the more committed I become to adhering to my own moral code and my own sense of what is meaningful, the stronger I become and the more free I become to act. Also the more joyful my life becomes.

The lesson has been that the more moral I am, the more healthful and fully realized a human I become, and vice versa. And the more healthy I become, the easier it is to live with constant happiness, to act effectively, to think and decide clearly, to see countless options and select and attain them. As in so many other aspects of life, it is a sort of counter-intuitive process: it is in accepting the limits of morality and meaning that one attains boundless freedom. Moral anarchy is imprisonment. Being emotionally and morally disconnected puts you in a cave, not on a higher plane.

Anyway, what I was trying to say is that it is reassuring to have a direct and wholesome reaction such as you had to the trapped mouse. It is like the world saying, "you're okay."

This may be one of those instances in which I assumed we were sharing, in years past, an experience, the feeling of emotional/moral disconnect, but you may not actually have been experiencing it. What say you?

I don't get the calculating/manipulative thing, but it sounds interesting. Can you elaborate? Regarding "I just have to make sure that my motives in my dealings with others are good ones," how about this:

> The only guide to a man is his conscience; the only shield to his memory is the rectitude and sincerity of his actions.
>
> Winston Churchill
> Their Finest Hour

I like the shield part. I don't have that now. When I look back on things I did wrong in the past, I often can't comfort myself that my actions were always moral and sincere, albeit mistaken or ineffective. I want to build that shield for my future, though, by acting always on principles, so that when my actions go astray, they will be mistakes rather than sins.

What is nice about these exchanges of ours is that it provides the opportunity and incentive for me to address the topics that I know should have precedence in my life, and which I resist taking the time to consider. My job is so hectic, and my home life as well, that I have to make a special effort to make time for anything that is optional, and I haven't made time for this. What folly! My life is so much happier than it was, yet a happy life can be as wrong a path as a sad one. More tolerable but also harder to look past, with less incentive to examine and change. Also, it seems to me that solitary thought is always ultimately misdirected. Any human mind pursuing a thread on its own eventually goes astray, sometimes subtly and horribly. So having the benefit of your thoughts is a corrective and enriching mechanism that is invaluable.

Regarding the B-52's first album, it is a staple of our family. Our kids love to dance to "Rock Lobster" and "Planet Clair." I would like to see the Shy Tuna.

Comments in your last couple messages make me realize I have expressed myself imperfectly. I do not advocate serenity, or withdrawing, or any kind of placidity or turning away from the world. I agree that you and I, probably you even more than I, have been far too good at withdrawing and being serene, to the point of hollowness. I advocate a more dynamic, outward-thrusting, active life than either of us was ever able to live before.

What I am saying is that the key to the ability to live that life is inside us, not in any scene, or style, or movement, or anything else "out there." It is not in experimenting with or trying on different attitudes or ideas or lifestyles or personae. I am saying that when we are grounded, solid, healthy people, we will find smiles on our faces, joy in our hearts, and a feeling of confidence and capability, and we will look around and the rich possibilities of life will open to us, and the paths to their attainment will appear at our feet. This can only be found within ourselves.

What concerned me is that the one message of yours made me wonder if you were looking at "out there" for ways to throw off the limits and shackles on your thoughts and actions, and in particular that you were looking at parts of "out there" that seem to me busy but sterile, when it seems to me that the more effective path is to look within yourself, to find your true self, to let go of all those external ideas, to become a unique and effective operating human unit. Maybe I was all wet, but that is what I was trying to get at. There is nothing in weird or fringe culture that offers anything that will do you any good. It is just another kind of useless conformity and prosaicness, which styles itself as nonconformist and unique. None of it is of value to somebody with your exceptional qualities. You are lucky enough to have a diamond mine in your soul, there is no use in you digging for brown coal in some counter culture.

Your comments on "the past 13 months" were interesting. It is hard for me to understand the impulses that drove you to get married again so quickly.* And it is difficult for me to understand your description of tearing off restraints and so forth. I know that you know what you are saying, and of course I can understand what you are saying in a sort of theoretical or abstract level, but it is hard for me to relate those concepts to the situation that I see you in. It seems that I am focusing on exploring and unleashing my inner abilities, and that I see my problem as an internal problem of having lacked the ability or capacity to think, act, and feel in the ways that I want to, while you are looking at it more as a problem of barriers or restraints or conventionality that you need to cast aside. It is just really hard for me to understand that your problem was one that can be addressed by "putting yourself at risk" or "taking chances." I'm not being critical, I just genuinely don't get it. To me, it looks like you are trading a box for a cage, or a straitjacket for a leash. Maybe you can make me see this some other way, we are just on a disconnect here.

Also, my puzzlement about your marriage does not mean that I would have expected you or wanted you to live a "footloose, bohemian lifestyle" as a single man instead. Quite the contrary! Your current lifestyle and thinking are more bohemian and footloose than I would have imagined you seeking! I guess my unthinking assumption would have been that after exiting your prior marriage so adroitly, you would take some time to simply become yourself, to become a healthy and fully realized Kevin, and that you would then be in a position to marry, or do anything else you chose to do, from a strong vantage point. This isn't anything I really thought about, I wasn't really thinking about you getting remarried at all, I suppose. However, my vision of your single life was the opposite of bohemian; more in the neighborhood of a wholesome period in which you could establish an emotional base and a vision of the future. A time to breathe some clean air, and make unfettered decisions, I guess.

In the course of this recent exchange I have come to see that my greatest threat is to "settle in" to this pleasant life too completely. I want this to be a solid launchpad for the rest of my life, not a comfortable wagon rut. I hope you will continue to spur me to continue to question and examine the assumptions and convention we live with. I don't want to put fetters on my future that are self-imposed and illusory. As you say, it is only too easy for me, as well as for you, maybe even more so, to only see a narrow range of options, to not nourish the capacity to see or create opportunities for radical innovation.

I certainly do appreciate your kind words. It is difficult for me to see how you get that much from me, when I don't really feel like I am giving much to you, and particularly when I feel that so much of what I say to you must have the quality of an irritating whine, but it is nice to be told. I do love you very much. You are in a category of one in my life.

I just about wet my pants when I read about the positive response from that editor. Could it really happen? It's one of those things you don't really even dare to hope for, like winning Publisher's Clearing House.

Re: the Churchill quote, I know Reagan D will make some bad decisions and suffer. It is his mode of living. I suspect the girls will, too. Of course, everyone will. But it is painful to anticipate, as you say.

How can I explain a curious phenomenon? We exchange deeply intimate thoughts in e-mail and conversations. We are very close. And yet I sense an opaqueness to you. In years past, I felt barriers. As I once explained, I had the sensation that you had internal compartments, and I only had access to certain ones. That you used different compartments to interact with different people or to accomplish different purposes. Like a submarine with sealable bulkheads, you could travel to different parts of your internal self, sealing hatches behind you as you went. It enabled you to live in trying circumstances without having aspects of yourself destroyed by exposure to inhospitable or inconsistent realities. You were careful about what awarenesses or ideas you allowed to move from one compartment to another. I was aware that when I asked something that would make you call on data from another compartment, there was this change in your voice, like you were scanning the ideas you might have to retrieve from elsewhere to see if they were compatible with the consciousness you maintained in the compartments I interacted with, and then you would give me this sort of translated/evasive version that was adapted to the environment.

Everyone does this to some extent, we are all somewhat different people depending on the company and the situation, and that is just a necessary human tool, but it may be that you attained an exaggerated version of this internal mechanism. I never really minded. I never really even thought about it much, until you moved out and got divorced, and it all started opening up. Then I could see the contrast. It was becoming that I was relating to Kevin in toto, and it was great. You seemed so much more integrated, also more natural and authentic, more direct, you even began to have moods, albeit mild ones.

Now, increasingly over the past year, it is back to the compartment feeling. To some extent I'm sure that's just normal. After all, a person does have to save some intimate and private part of himself for his romantic partner. Even close others can't really be let into that chamber. But it makes me worry that maybe you are going back to a compartmental life. The danger of that is, that some of one's compartments can go and do really stupid things, without the other compartments really even being conscious of it or having control over it.

I know how that works, believe me. It's like there is at least one part of yourself that you can hand the reins to when it's time to make a really bad decision that you don't want to admit to yourself, or tell others about. I've done that. There is an aspect to you that has an impulse to secretiveness. I sense that you have a basement in yourself that you go off to in order to make decisions and plans. As close as we are, I have always had the feeling from you that I shouldn't push into that realm. Maybe I am doing that now, and shouldn't. I always understood, on some inarticulable level, why you never went for counseling or therapy. I knew it was really no good to tell you to do it. You handle private things like that inside yourself, all alone.

I had a friend like that in college. We got very close, but at some point I realized he was not really open to me. He would send me very intimate messages from his basement self, but they were still being thrown over a wall. The barrier was always there, the editing process remained to select what would be allowed to be released. Interestingly, like you he was perceived by those who knew him as exceptionally warm, kind, understanding, patient, and he never had moods. I knew better, about him and about you.

To me, that closed and secret approach seems like a dangerous life strategy. As I observed above, any human being thinking through something alone will eventually go wrong, and sometimes dangerously wrong. I think in the past you have perceived and pursued paths to enlightenment and wisdom that proved illusory, even harmful. Of course anyone can do that, and most people do. I may be doing that now, for all I know. However, although I know you will always be a deeply private person, you may find benefit in making your decisions and forming your thoughts more out in the sunlight. If you had been willing to bounce your ideas off other people more, then maybe by getting a reaction from other people, you could have been spared going down some bad roads in the past. I have never pried into that stuff. But I have the sense that at different times in the past you have had a plan that was going to solve your problems and lead to great things for you, but actually it was hare-brained.

I have learned myself, that if I am hesitating to share an idea or plan with others, that is a strong sign that some part of me knows it's wrong or stupid and that I don't want to be told that. I worry right now, to be frank, that you may be forming some ideas or making some plans that are self-deceptive and dopey. I worry this because, even though we do engage in these very personal communications, I have this idea that you are keeping key stuff under wraps.

January 1996: Spontaneous Long Impassioned Message

I don't really know what your situation is. For example, Mom and I didn't really hear much about Deborah at all until you told us you were engaged. Now an adult man does not need to consult with anyone before proposing marriage, of course. But it makes me wonder if some part of you did not want to be told not to do it, did not want to be told it was too soon and just not wise. You knew you wanted to do it, and didn't want to have to scrutinize the decision.

I suppose I am hitting pretty close to home here. I'm sorry. No good ever comes of meddling with another's marriage. I remember I predicted to you that you would soon find yourself living in a very small world. You were quite strong that you would not let that happen. And believe me, I have noticed this incredible effort and outpouring on your part to maintain and even expand on the communication and closeness between us, and I love it!

A friend of mine once told me that when he found himself in emotional trouble or pain, he called everyone he knew. That amazed me. My response was always to crawl quickly to an internal cave and keep it a secret from everyone. I saw that his path was not my natural instinct, but that it was better, and have tried to train myself to follow it, although of course not to quite that extreme. Our whole family has this terrible flaw of always maintaining this "I'm all OK" facade, and deeming it too impolite to question each other on whether it's really true. I don't want to follow that pattern anymore. It's safe, but arid. For example, you have alluded to being in a sort of financial pinch. Now in Annie's family, they would pry all the details loose, and then if the situation merited it, everyone would call around and they would send that person whatever money they could spare. I, on the other hand, am too polite to inquire. It's the Pufall way, and it stinks.

To me, if there are constraints that are inhibiting you in life, they may not be constraints of conventionality or constraints of not questioning common assumptions, etc. but rather constraints, invisible to you, in how you view yourself. When I was down there for the wedding, it struck me that I see you differently than some of the people down there do. And then it occurred to me later that maybe I see you differently than you see yourself.

You have to understand my childhood experience. You were always better than me at everything that mattered, and NOT just because you were older. When you ran races, you won blue ribbons. When I ran races, I was just barely in ribbon contention. Similarly, you won blue or purple ribbons for your artwork, while I might get the occasional red or white. At any game or sport, you were more gifted. You were better looking, funnier, kinder, more considerate, better behaved with Mom, braver, and so forth.

Now maybe I hit on some things, like debate and speaking, in which I was more gifted than you, but that was when I was older and you had left for school. It just cracks me up to see now, as I just think I saw down there at the wedding, that some people see me as "the successful brother." I mean, I had some lucky breaks, and I gutted some things out, and I ended up with a couple of degrees, and that's it, that's all the difference. And it was close! A few close calls going the other way and I wouldn't have those. And similarly, you were just that close the other way. A few little breaks, a few minor choices, and it would be you with the PhD or whatever.

I know the reality here, I know who you are and who I am. For at least the first 16 years of my life I lived with the constant experience that you were better at everything, and really, were just a more gifted person than I. And it is also true that you absorbed many psychic blows that would otherwise have fallen more heavily on me, and that you willingly incurred damage that decreased the damage done to me. I have always, at first unconsciously and later consciously, acknowledged my lasting debt, or at least recognition and gratitude, to you for that service. I have never, or at least not since I was very young, felt any resentment for your gifts or guilt for the damage you suffered on my behalf. I always took pleasure in the glory of your giftedness and your achievements, and I have always felt grateful for, rather than guilty about, the huge favor you did in serving as a partial shield during my childhood.

I believe that is how you would have wanted it, because if I crippled myself with guilt, your sacrifice would have been in vain, which I think would be really irritating and frustrating. Those blows you took for me may well be why I have a JD and you didn't get your BS, personally I tend to believe that. Now this does not mean that I have you up on a pedestal in some idealized way, it's just that I see you, and will always see you, as a tremendously strong, capable, talented person. Now of course the damage you incurred growing up screwed you up and screwed up your life. You determined not to succeed, and you consigned yourself to life's margins. I did the same, only less so, in accordance with my relatively sheltered position and my somewhat different individual natural response to the same stimulus. So most of the people who have known you have not seen who you are. Perhaps you do not see who you are, or who you were meant to be.

One big favor you could do yourself is to make up your mind right now that you are not going to try to be, and shouldn't be, as nice and considerate as you have pretended to be all these years. You are an exceptionally nice, kind, considerate, thoughtful, and gentle person. That is all good, but it is not at the heart of who you are, and you even though you are awful damn nice, you are not as nice as you have been acting all these years, because no one is that nice. Also, as nice as you have acted, it is not entirely genuine. You have seen how Annie reacts to your niceness. It drives her nuts. It's like a dog whistle to her. Her instinctive reaction is to try to goad you, to try to break through that patina to what's real. You may have noticed that she is often a pain in the ass around you, almost to an irrational degree. Now I am not commending her behavior, but I think that is the root cause. She doesn't like the candy coating.

I am not saying you should turn mean, that wouldn't be you either. I mean, I'm convinced that you are really a good and kind person, but it will be even better when it's just the real you. You won't be the moodless wonder any more, nor as flawlessly considerate, but it will probably actually be more comfortable to those around you. I know people have always been uncomfortable with me, because as polite and considerate as I always am, on some level they smell plastic, and it makes them uneasy and distrustful. I'd rather be a little less seamless and a lot more real.

I advise shock therapy: for the next month, don't open a door for ANYONE (I mean anyone!) unless she is carrying a package with both hands. Resolve that for the rest of your life, when you are approaching a parked car with another person, you will unlock YOUR door, get in, reach over, and unlock the other door, rather than open their door for them and then go around and get in yours. At least once a week, decline to do something for someone because it would be inconvenient for you to do so. You get the idea.

Consider the character in your book, Wes. He doesn't have a single honest relationship. He is incapable of it. And he has no idea that this is unusual, he doesn't even perceive it. Wes is locked away in a completely closed internal compartment. When he has to relate to someone, it is always completely artificial. He goes through a rapid internal process of deciding how this person expects him to react, and then simulates that reaction. His treatment of everyone in his life is entirely secretive and manipulative. He never makes a decision, exerts any control over his life, or exhibits a genuine emotion. Everything is screened going in and coming out. He tries to manipulate others to avoid having to confront unpleasant emotions, but he will unthinkingly do whatever he perceives those around him expect him to do. In other words, his two modes are amoral manipulation to avoid conflict, and unthinking conformity. He is an empty vessel. He remains so at the end of the book. He is unchanged, and he is doomed.

Now that I re-read that paragraph, it didn't quite go where I wanted it to. I am not saying you are doomed, or an empty vessel. But this quality of the real person being so strongly isolated internally, and relating to others in a conscious and artificial mode, as though across a distance or through a barrier, is something to consider. Because the book does not present Wes as being an unusual and dysfunctional character. The assumption is that readers will relate to this method of living, that they will be able to envision themselves operating as he does. This makes me wonder if, to some extent, this is the way life looks from inside Kevin.

I used to sometimes get the sense, for example, that you would get on the phone with me, to change some plans for some reason, and you would sort of start talking around something until I would see what I was supposed to say, that I would volunteer to change some date or something, but really, I would just wish you would have come right out with it. And I catch myself doing it, just sort of broaching some topic from the side, getting a sense of how the other person might react, tailor my message accordingly, and so forth. I think people hate that. Anyway, I'm getting way off the point here. I don't even know what my point was anymore.

Let's try this: Who are you? You're nice, but that's not what you're about. And I don't think your mission or your gift is to be a warm counselor type thing. Deep down, I think you're really a bit cold hearted, as I am, because you see things and people as they are. Your analysis is too keen to be entirely warm. I mean, I am turning out to be a much nicer person than I ever thought I was, but you can't cut to the core and still be fuzzy. Annie did me a big goddamn favor a long time ago when she told me, and kept telling me when I didn't believe her, that I am a Type-A Male, an assertive, competitive, achieving guy. Now having grown up with you and Mom, I am a kinder and gentler Type A, but that's what's at the core, or at least that's a rough description of a big chunk of it. The more I let me be myself, and let go of all the baggage, the more of that comes through. And I think it's coming through in a pretty good way, all in all.

So what are you? Are you an analyzer? A chronicler? A dissector? Is it your nature to see deeply and set forth what you see, to reveal to others the hidden aspects of our lives? Is that what you're heading for with your writing, the perceiving and uncovering of truths, even in, maybe especially in, your fiction? That's what Calvin and Hobbes did, that made it so special, so much better than most other cartoons, and funnier. I don't know. Is that it? Maybe there is no "it." Or at least no single "it." All I know is, you have to become yourself, and I am very eager to be with you and know you. I wish we lived in the same city.

I think it is possible that as part of your self-destructive response to your childhood, you identified yourself with the fringe, and developed an interest in the weird, the occult, etc. This always seemed like a fruitless impulse, and one that was unworthy of you. That's all just a bunch of shit, you know. Being into offbeat stuff is about as interesting and challenging and nonconformist and mind-expanding as being into Republicanism. You won't find yourself or anything else of value there.

Of course, I should talk. I found valuable nuggets of insight in the commercialized pablum of a self-promoting quasi–New Age enlightenment guru. So I'm not consistent. Sue me! All I'm saying is, you should be way past that. I kind of wonder if some big part of you went into an emotional deep freeze at some point, and that now you are picking up where you left off.

May I be blunt? This idea of exploring alternative ideas, tearing off the constraints of convention, putting yourself at risk reminds me of the college sophomore/junior time frame. I mean, if you have to take yourself through that, then you have to do that, and that's fine, but if I am perceiving this correctly and that's what's happening here, then also step back and take some perspective. It's a phase. It won't satisfy you. You are too good for that. You belong in the middle of the big stream of life, not off in some fruitless eddy. You are more than strong enough to swim the big current. Those people who are into that stuff can't hack the real ideas. The real history of our age is being written in Discover magazine, which give us an accessible version of the uncovering of new real knowledge and abilities. It is being written by people like Jon Hassler who chronicle the real lives we are living, who are making an intimate and perceptive record of who we are and how we live. Pop culture and counter culture and all that is trash. Your mind deserves to be grappling with the real thing.

You need to get yourself together. I think, personally, that you are one and a half baby steps down the road to being a healthy you, just like me. Hey, they are important steps, but it's just the start! You can't do what you need to do, not like you should be doing it, until you let some more crap go and do some more filling in FROM THE INSIDE. You'll know when you're solid. These ideas you're trying on now, they're baby stuff. Maybe the real you will always be interested in exploring the fringe, maybe that is part of who you are, and then, I can live with that, but when you were out on your own there for a while, that's NOT where I saw you going. You deserve to be in the middle of the big world, living a big life, not off on the sides. You say you still have this resistance to success and so forth, and I agree, and I think maybe it's got the upper hand right now! I still say you looked you real life in the eye, and blinked. But that's okay, we all blink, shit I've been looking at the road I KNOW I need to take and I've been blinking like a 1963 debutante with first generation contact lenses!

I don't have any idea anymore where I am going with any of this. It's past my bedtime and I'm here at my office just pounding this stuff out from the heart. I hope it makes some kind of sense, and I sure as hell hope I haven't stepped way over some line here, because I don't EVER want to screw up our relationship. I just think you're at the crossroads of Glory Street and Oblivion Avenue and I sure don't want you to go the wrong way.

I'm not trying to tell you how to run your life. You obviously have plans you've made and ideas you've formulated, and goodness knows, I mean, you did write a goddamn book and so forth, so why should I be questioning it. Except I just have this gnawing feeling and I just couldn't keep my mouth shut about it. I can't pretend that when I look at what you're doing that I'm not concerned. I feel like I've said too much, but that there is so much I didn't say or didn't say well enough. I just went back and re-read this tome, and it's like I'm just dancing around whatever it is I'm trying to tell you. It felt so right as I typed it, and now I can't tell if any of it's true, or if it's just pretentious bullshit. And I don't want you to feel like you don't dare say anything to me for fear I'm going to go stew on it and blow it all out of proportion and then dump all over you. Jesus, I wish we lived in the same town.

As is reflected in several emails, I was baffled and concerned about Kevin's decision to remarry relatively quickly. I needn't have worried. Deborah turned out to be a wonderful person and their marriage has been a remarkably happy one.

* * *

Date: 1/16/96
From: Reagan
Subject: Was in a deep, deep well

How fleeting these victories can be. Just yesterday I had a very unpleasant episode in which all progress seemed illusory.* I hope we can continue to communicate about these matters and that I can get input to keep the fires burning.

It would be safe to say that at that point in time the Bureau was one of the most reviled institutions in the state, so we were on the receiving end of continual hostility and criticism, often from the very people we were working hard to serve. We had no previous experience in the insurance industry or as managers, so we were experimenting and figuring out what worked as we went. Naturally there were setbacks, sometimes truly dismaying ones. If only we could have known then how well it would all work out in the end!

* * *

Date: 1/17/96
From: Reagan
Subject: Another great idea!

I had this idea for an article some time ago. It is probably unpublishable, and it may just be stupid, but it has sort of stuck with me, and so I thought I would share it.

The title would be important, but I can't quite get it right. Some of the possibilities:

Everything You Know Is Wrong
or
The New Truths

So the article would just be a series of statements. The article could probably not have a single point. If it were satirical in a single-minded way, on a single theme, it would get boring fast. I would have to be provocative, and maybe should keep the reader guessing on which statements were sincere and which satirical, and which in between. I generally don't think scattershot "provocativeness" is worth much, but there you go. You could organize it by themes, or do it randomly. A sample:

Any great book was actually written by a woman. Any great painting was actually painted by a woman. Jesus was a woman. Human society was and will be matriarchal. Masculine values are false. Nothing can be achieved by greater effort. The government is an evil conspiracy. There is a hidden power controlling human events. Our first president was an imposter serving the Illuminati. Thomas Jefferson grew marijuana for smoking. The collapse of communism is a ruse. Western ideas are false. Your religious beliefs are false. Crystals contain hidden powers. Great events will occur with the beginning of the new century. Terrible calamities will occur with the beginning of the new century. What children see and hear on television and in movies does not affect them. If you don't approve of what is being shown on television, you can turn it off. The generation born in the Seventies is unmotivated and amoral. There is no difference between great art and popular art. Great art is dead. The world is getting smaller. The world is fragmenting. The truth is within us all. All prophets were great teachers. All prophets are dead white males. Religion is a tool of male domination. Religion is and will be matriarchal. God is a woman. God has no gender. The women apostles have been hidden from us.

This would have to be reorganized to make it work better. We could just both accumulate these things over time and then play with them. What would be great is if it could have a sort of subtle rhythm, you know? The trick would be to keep people reading.

* * *

Date: 1/18/96
From: Kevin
Subject: Good stuff

Tonight's background music: Talking Heads, Popular Favorites, Disc Two. I wish the liner notes came with lyrics.

Sorry to hear about the low time. I think you've had quite enough of that for a while. The potential for a crash occurred on my end a few days ago. Peggy called to tell me that the icemaker I had hooked up for them had leaked, causing damage to walls and ceilings downstairs and the hardwood floor upstairs. I could feel all the old monsters readying themselves to pounce, to make me feel inept, unreliable, withdrawn. But I fought back. I've found it helpful to think of the Churchill biography at times like that, to consider the tremendous disasters that were a part of his life as well as the amazing triumphs. Talk about putting things in perspective. I've also benefited from considering how Gerry Goodwin might react in a similar situation, which is, as far as I understand him, to focus all of his energies on solving the problem, and not waste any time beating up on himself.

Most importantly, I didn't want to let it throw my writing off. I'd been working to get a new draft of the book in the mail to the agent (I hope I can say "my agent" soon), and I was afraid that my inner requirements for successful writing would be easily overwhelmed be an occurrence that was hammering at my sense of self-worth. What I found was that the compartmentalization that you've referred to (more on that later) was a very helpful concept in this instance. I did what I could to fix the problem I had created, then closed the door on that area and went to work on the writing. I result was some of the most productive time that I've spent on the book. I was up until 7 a.m. one night, working creatively the whole time.

Another aspect of the situation was the emotional part. I was deeply dismayed on first hearing what had happened, and eventually it started turning into anger, the kind of hard-to-direct anger you get when you hit your head on something: "I'm REALLY PISSED OFF here! I'd like to KICK SOMEONE'S ASS!" In the past, I would have directed all of that inwards and added it to the big, twisted ball of sickness there. I wondered this time about "using the anger" to inspire my writing, an idea which didn't really appeal to me for some reason, but what I found was that I could use the anger to help me in a subtly different way, to increase my desire to succeed. In a way, I turned the anger back on itself.

I know, I know, you're thinking "He shouldn't have been hooking up the icemaker in the first place! He's being too helpful and then beating up on himself for an honest mistake!" Well, yes, I was being helpful, but I REALLY LIKE doing stuff like that, the home handyman type jobs. Sue me.

I wish the damage hadn't happened, of course, but I have learned from it. I addition to what I've already said, I had another welcome revelation: that I had only a fleeting desire to withdraw, to swear off further helpful activities just because one of them went sour. I feel willing to live fully, as I desire, while accepting that sometimes the results may not be what I expected or intended. (More on helpfulness later.)

Speaking of what I desire, this seems like a good point to return to the subject of my lifestyle choices of the past year. I still feel that I haven't adequately communicated my point of view to you. One aspect of my decision to marry again so quickly is this: I've lived a lot of my life regretting the past, suffering through the present and fantasizing about the future. None of that was healthy. These days, I feel much more comfortable about the past (seeing the progress that I've made and having learned from the hard times and mistakes), I'm really enjoying the present, and I'm looking forward to and working productively to improve the future.

Part of enjoying the present (and this may sound cold, but it's not) is the fulfillment of my needs and desires on a daily basis. I'm willing to work and wait to achieve some of my goals, but I don't want to put off enjoying what life has to offer right now, and Deborah has a lot to offer me, right now, in addition to having a capacity for growing and changing along with me. She's the best cuddler I've ever snuggled up to. She's very easy to live with day-to-day. She likes new experiences and enjoys keeping active, but also has a wonderful capacity for relaxation and quiet time. She's very supportive and encouraging of my work. She's easy to talk to, especially about emotional issues. Her innate gentleness and kindness have helped me to explore some very sensitive areas inside myself.

But, all of this may be irrelevant to you (not at all meant in a bad way). I value your perspectives and insights a great deal, and it continues to mystify and worry me that you and I seem to hold such divergent views on the course that my recent life should have taken. Over the years, you've been right on the money in identifying my self-deceptions and poor life-choices. I've usually, on some level, known that you were right at the time, and have later seen clearly that I was fooling myself, but right now, no matter how objective and self-analyzing I try to be, I don't feel that I've taken a wrong turn or missed an opportunity.

So, what's going on? Options: 1. I've reached a new and subtle level of nearsightedness or self-deception. 2. You had a vision of my future that was understandable, logical, and attractive, but didn't incorporate some key factors unique to my situation. 3. It could be somewhere in the middle, with my choice being not as wise as it seems to me right now, but not as big a failure as you might fear. Let's go on to something else for a bit, and return to this when I start commenting on your massive opus.

Look to the mail, my son, look to the mail. Amusement is on its way.

Well, I certainly found your article idea to be a stimulating one. I think you're right about it needing a rhythm, or rhythms, and it feels like there are all kinds of possibilities there: a series of contrasting pairs, gradations from one extreme to another, wildly random mixes, subtle commentary punctuated by eye-popping fabrication . . . let's see what I can do with this. I recall writing down a few similar statements a long time ago: Mary Poppins was a witch; Realtors sell houses, not homes. It'll be fun thinking about this.

So, I got "Little Witch" mailed off today, and I'm going to focus on the depression self-help book next. Tentative title: "First Aid for Depression: What to do when you feel helpless." My potential agent recommended a particular book on writing book proposals, so I went to the bookstore and looked through it and got some good information. (Ironic, huh? Here I am, trying to sell me stuff, and I'm stiffing the author of a book on how to sell my stuff.)

So, on to your novella (I hope you have a copy to refer to).

As we discussed on the phone, I think that "sociopath" is a useful word in a broader sense than the dictionary definition I quoted. So, let's just decide that that's how we want to use it.

I found your views on morality and freedom to be thought-provoking. Hmm . . . that sounds trite. ("How did you find your steak, sir?" "How did I find my steak? I LOOKED UNDER MY DINNER ROLL, that's how I found my steak!") Anyway, I must admit to feeling somewhat unsettled in that area. I think that it's part of my overall desire to question standards and assumptions and allow myself to think widely and freely. The idea of what constitutes moral thought and behavior is as open to question as anything else right now. As I'm writing this, it sounds juvenile. Is it, as you have sometimes theorized, a picking up of my life where I left it during my depression? I think that's part of it, but the other part is a desire to fully explore the possibilities of my new vocation and, beyond that, to live a life as far above normal as it was below previously. I'd very much like to find out more about what your moral code consists of and how it developed.

To me, it sounds as though we've had similar experiences regarding feelings of disconnection and detachment. What you referred to as your "power" and "edge" seem similar to what I was describing as feeling "calculating" and "manipulative" – a potentially unhealthy and immoral use of knowledge and insight. As to what constitutes "good motives," that sounded vague even as I wrote it. The fact is, I truly enjoy looking into the hearts and minds of others, and have approached this activity with the intention of making my life, and their lives, richer. Looking back, I feel pretty good about my dealings with people, and fairly satisfied that I've made positive contributions to the lives that have intersected mine (leaving aside the sometimes tremendous negatives that arose as a result of my poor emotional health).

I, too, am very pleased to have you as a thought-partner. Thinking new thoughts, examining ideas and beliefs, questioning the direction of my life; these are very important to me, and much easier to do with you as critic, supporter, and collaborator.

Regarding the idea of serenity. I feel much more serene now that I'm living a more dynamic life (particularly an internally dynamic life). What I had achieved previously, and which could be mistaken for serenity, was placidity.

I realize that the important stuff, the growth, the thought, the creativity, goes on inside me, but, as you said in your comments about solitary thought, outside influences are a necessity. Just as we need the future to keep the present dynamic, we need the stimulation of the outside world to keep us growing. Of course, with the tremendous range and volume of such stimulation that's available these days, the question of what to seek out and what to allow inside you becomes a big one. I don't feel like getting into that one right now.

In reading what you wrote about "exploring and unleashing my inner abilities," it sounds like we're in somewhat similar frames of mind. That statement could apply to me as well as to you. But when you stated that ". . . I see my problem as an internal problem of having lacked the ability or capacity to think, act and feel in the ways that I want to . . ." I wonder if I'm going beyond that to ask, "How will I know what I want until I know what is possible?" The barriers of conventionality are as much my own habitual and ignorant limitations of thought and feeling as they are externally imposed ones.

As for "taking chances," one example occurred while I was working on my book some months ago, when I dug so deep emotionally during one scene that I had to stop writing and go lie down with Deborah for a while for comfort. This may not sound like much, but had voluntarily entered a very dark place in myself in order to create, and you know how terrifying those places can be. I don't have the desire to wallow in the shadows while working or living, but I also don't want to shy away from challenges on any front.

The idea of becoming "healthy and fully realized," unfettered by the restrictions and demands of a committed relationship – to me, this has some of the elements of the "solitary thought" idea. I know how important it is to have a strong, healthy sense of self, and I've been developing that over the course of the past few years. I continue to grow in that way today. However, and this goes back to my "placidity," I had lived for most of my life with an unhealthy, illusory, and unworkable desire to be complete in myself, which I have sometimes heard as the stated goal of self-esteem programs, but which really leads to sterility and isolation. What I really needed was to learn how to be a strong me in the context of a life lived fully in the world, which, in large part, means a life lived in close relationship with others. I'm satisfied that I'm capable of living successfully on my own, in a practical sense, and I enjoyed my interlude of bachelor life, but I can't and don't want to, live happily outside of a loving, dynamic relationship.

Related to this is my longstanding tendency to want to accomplish things without assistance, in order to get a greater feeling of pride and so that I wouldn't have to share the rewards. The biggest example of this is my unwillingness to seek professional help over the years. "I overcame it myself. Pretty amazing, aren't I?" Of course, I was very lucky to have you to assume the role of counsellor, and (not intended as a criticism of your efforts) it did take seventeen years of my adult life to beat that condition. It's not necessarily a bad thing, seeing what you can accomplish on your own, but in my case the desire isn't entirely constructive. I want to feel free to intermingle my life with others', to not worry about who gets the credit and the blame.

Should I just come out and say, "I love her, and that's the only reason anyone needs."? A small part of me keeps nagging me to do so, but you and I know that it won't do. I did fall in love with her, and I do love her, and our love continues to grow and deepen, but you and I, like just about everyone else, had been fooled by love, and I know it takes more than that to create a lasting relationship. That's why I've been trying to describe for you what she does for me and how she has contributed to my growth.

I'll do my best to keep you unsettled – in the most positive way possible, of course. And even if I wasn't, I have a feeling that you don't have it in you to stop growing. You're much too dynamic internally.

Opaqueness & barriers . . . I seem to be hitting a sleep barrier at this time. I'll continue tomorrow.

Boy, did you write a long message!

* * *

Date: 1/18/96
From: Reagan
Subject: Has his fingertips on the rim of the wall

So now the kids are getting to compound problems in math in school. Somehow I got to thinking about what compound problems in other subjects might look like. Here is a compound problem for a course in Zen:

"If a tree falls in the forest, and there is no one there to hear it, does it make more or less noise than the sound of one hand clapping? Show your work."

I haven't gotten "Popular Favorites" because I have the idea that I am going to buy all their albums over time. But will I? WILL I?

I can certainly relate to the leaking ice maker scenario. And no, I actually wasn't really thinking "What was he doing hooking it up in the first place, he's being too helpful." You're good at that kind of thing, and it's a genuinely nice thing to do. How did Peggy take it? When someone does you a favor that goes awry, the obligation is to make them very comfortable with the situation. I can certainly understand why you are feeling what you are feeling, because it's just how I would react. Don't you think that it is just a maybe exaggerated version of how anyone would feel about it? I suppose the challenge for us is to bring our guilt/self-recrimination down into the normal range.

You know, as I read your message I can imagine exactly how I would feel, which is pretty much how I guess you were feeling, and I can also imagine just about exactly what the "healthy" alternative emotional response would be, and it would be so easy to be glib and just say "choose to feel this way about it," either to you or to myself, but it's not really that easy.

Although, it's funny, because when I am living in the right mode, it actually is easy, in fact effortless, to react to things in a healthy way instead of in the bad ingrained old ways.

It must be a subtle and difficult challenge to not let things like that set back your writing. I mean, it's hard enough for me, and I have the benefit of set hours, and people who would notice if I didn't get my work done, and so forth. This is sort of a switcheroo from our previous respective jobs in this respect.

Your reaction of not withdrawing from being helpful because one project went bad does seem like a useful Churchillian reaction. He made the calls and took the ones that worked out and the ones that didn't and went right along. You're right, that is a really good reaction that I am going to be mulling over for my own use. Is it the opposite of "once burned, twice shy?"

I found your comments on your marriage to be reassuring, not that I have any real right to be reassured or not reassured about it.

I like the realtors one. How about "maternal instinct is a myth," or "humans are not monogamous by nature."

You certainly know how to use capitalization to good effect. I don't seem to be able to underline or bold or anything like that in these messages. Doesn't that seem unfortunate? If e-mail is going to be a prominent mode of interpersonal communication, it will need to accommodate the broadest possible ranges of nuance and emphasis. Conventions could develop. Like, italics denote irony.

Like you, I would also like to find out what my moral code consists of and how it developed.

Hah! Or as they say on the internet ;)

Apparently my moral code does not preclude the use of hackneyed sarcasm in a lame attempt to humorously deflect a serious inquiry. So there's a start! Anything else you want to know about it?

One thing I'm pretty sure of, my moral code is not embodied it the Cub Scout Oath to any meaningful degree. Details to follow.

You must have your message for reference to understand the following comments:

Leaving "that" aside, I've done pretty well too, but, at least in my case, that's a pretty damn big aside.

Oooh! Nice distinction between serenity and placidity!

Good point on limits of conventionality being as much internal as external. Actually, you've hit on what I have recognized since I wrote (or as I wrote) my message as a sore point for me: that I am accepting without even perceiving a vast body of assumptions and constraints that limit my perceptions, my thoughts, my choices, and my actions. So maybe this limit burster thing you were talking about is something I should adopt rather than criticize.

Nice point also on the falseness of the goal of being complete unto yourself. Although that's a tough one. I mean, I think we do need to be self-sufficient in certain key respects, but also that we are meant to be interdependent creatures. I think this area needs close and careful examination, but I don't have the time for it right at the moment. I know I want my beliefs and goals and so forth to come from within me, and I don't want to live subject to judgements and reactions of others, but as I explained much too forcefully in my last message, the path of being too internal and cut-off is equally unhealthy. I'm just not in the right mode for picking this apart. I'm making way too many tough judgement calls all day long in my job, and my brain is just worn out from it.

It's interesting, but I had never picked up on the "pride of accomplishment" aspect of your impulse to fly solo. It just shows how easy it is to overlook or misperceive stuff in this area of analyzing or understanding how a person works or why a person has some behavior. I have been on both sides of the experience of realizing that a longstanding assumption about why somebody behaves a certain way or what a person is like is just turned 180 degrees in one disconcerting moment just based on some chance comment or some brief statement or explanation.

Despite my earlier comments on the ice maker incident, you must bear in mind that I am the final arbiter of how nice is too nice, and you must submit all your actions for my review.

I really can't imagine why I went off on such a tangent on that niceness thing. I think you should be just as nice as you can. Everyone should.

Subject to my review, of course.

That would have been a real snappy way to end this message, but I've had a thought. I really didn't mean to say that you were too nice, but that sometimes (sometimes!) your niceness seemed like a form of self-denial. The self-denial thing is interesting, it is something I have long perceived in you in the past, and have recently been surprised to discover that I have needed to deal with it myself as well! More later.

* * *

Date: 1/18/96
From: Reagan
Subject: is too quick with the send button

I did it again! Can you send that last one back to me? Thanks.

* * *

Date: 1/22/96
From: Kevin
Subject: Me

Well, I've tried and tried to write a response on the issue of opaqueness and compartmentalization a couple of times and failed. You make some good points and have led me to some good thinking, but I can't form a coherent reply yet.

I do feel much less likely to withdraw when in trouble, and it feels good. I maintain much more contact with others than I used to and have benefited in many ways. As for finances, if I really needed help and knew that you had help to give, I'd certainly ask for it. Hey, if you ever want to know how I'm doing, ask me. I have no secrets from you there.

Very interesting comments about viewpoint. I never saw myself as being innately better than you at anything, just older. It always seemed to me that you were better at things than I had been at your age, and that you did things, like music and debate, that I hadn't done at all. This idea was reinforced during your college career, with sports (fencing and basketball), drama and the enormous fact that you got a degree at all. And as far as absorbing blows, I really admired you for standing up to Dad as much as you did, at great emotional risk to yourself, while I shrunk away more and more. I thought that that said a lot about the basic kind of person you were.

Niceness: more food for thought. I think you're right, that most of it is real and part of it is affectation. The problem is, it's all so much habit that it may take some thought to tell the two apart. I will say this: women seem very appreciative of a male who is still at least somewhat guided by old ideas of civility. Still, I like the idea of examining an aspect of my life that I can't remember considering before. Like any other behavior or pattern of thinking, I want to look at it and make a decision.

As for Wes, he's Wes, not me. I started out with a character similar to myself, but he changed, and became much more unpleasant than I had intended. He's more like who I was than who I am, but still not identical.

I don't feel the need for subtle maneuvering anymore, and if you sense that I'm still doing it, I'd like to hear about it.

So, who am I, down deep? Does seeing deep into people (and I'm not sure that I do, although I'd like to) preclude being "nice" or "warm," or make the niceness less genuine? Maybe it does, I don't know. This, too, needs more thought.

Middle vs. fringe of life: part of that depends on your definitions. Middle can mean average, normal, well-known . . . which I am trying to avoid, or it can mean fully engaged and open to all options, which I like. When I think of being on the fringe, to me it means being creative, in thought and action, not being caught in some tiny, lunatic fantasy. Still, I'm not as adamant as you in rejecting some beliefs or ways of thinking. I've had enough changes of heart and mind over the years to be wary of absolute condemnation or affirmation.

Don't ever worry about saying the wrong thing to me. I just don't think it's possible for you to do so, and I really do value your honest observations of my life. I always trust you to have my best interests at heart and to say what you say out of caring and love.

* * *

Date: 1/23/96
From: Kevin
Subject: Stuff for you to read

Okay, finally getting to your last message.

I really enjoyed your compound problem. It reminds me of the famous compound response: "Hey, does the Pope shit in the woods?"

Peggy was actually very pleasant about the whole ice maker mess. What I felt about it was pretty much self-generated, and I did end up turning it into a lesson on appropriate responses to stressful situations.

I look forward to your comments concerning the Cub Scout Oath. As I recall, it was basically "I wish there was some good reason to carry this knife around." You know what I miss? Uniforms. Fewer and fewer people want to wear uniforms as time passes, although in the case of fast-food workers, I can understand. Those used to be hideous.

But the Girl and Boy Scout uniforms were swell, and it seems as though the kids are missing something by either not wanting to wear or feeling uncomfortable wearing the full regalia. Maybe it's different up there and they still go all-out, but here it's basically a shirt and jeans. The last shirt that Emily showed me was just a sweatshirt with a Scouting logo on the front. I think there's something to be said for having made the outfits, especially for the girls, more suitable for physical activities, but they seem a lot less special than they used to.

Obviously, this relates to the de-uniforming of the country in general, and I suppose that that could have a positive humanizing effect, but it could also lead to a decreasing feeling of pride and professionalism in adults and a missing element of fun in the children. As for the adults, imagine what it would look like if police officers began showing up in jeans, sneakers and polo shirts with badges embroidered on the pockets. And as for the kids, I think it takes away some of the fun of being a group member. Remember how great it felt to belong to a club, especially the ones we made up?

And the more stuff we made up that was unique to the club, the better it was.

I think our new motto should be "Leaving that aside."

One more comment about my "break down the barriers" mode, which also relates to our discussion concerning how we perceived each other while we were growing up. I became aware, during the last few years of our imaginative childhood play, that you had a greater capacity for purely creative invention than I did. I could certainly expand upon and improve upon a story idea, but you had the ability to come up with the wholly new story to begin with. I've fought to reach that level (succeeding best, so far, with Rampant Rockets*), and my current phase is basically a continuation of that – a search for and a strengthening of my ability to create.

*A comic strip that I had created 15 years earlier and that I would feature in an "e-zine" of the same name a couple of years later.

* * *

Date: 1/23/96
From: Reagan
Subject: May have strep throat

Your response to the compound Zen question was actually perfect. Wouldn't it be great to have someone spring that question on you and then you come right back with that response. What an amazing topper! Especially since only really discerning observers would appreciate the full propriety of the response.

Here is the Cub Scout Oath: "I [state your name] promise to do my best, to do my duty, to God and my country, to help other people, and to obey the Law of the Pack." I have nothing against this oath, it's just that it doesn't do much to address the moral questions I am on the verge of considering. You might say "Reagan, did you really expect your moral questions to be answered by the Cub Scout Oath? What are you using for brains, low fat margarine or something?"

Well, not exactly. I mean, it's not like I was looking forward to learning what the oath was, it's just that I was conscious of a sense of disappointment when I read it. I don't think it really give a boy some nugget that will be very useful to hark back to in years to come. And it doesn't stimulate any creative or useful thinking it me, at a time when so many other things, even like advertising slogans as we discussed earlier, are sparking useful trains of thought for me.

The "do my best" part, while realistic, seems wimpy, and is pretty much a waste of space at most. It's like having a wedding vow acknowledging that if things don't work out we'll get divorced. It's realistic, but it's still not a good idea. I mean, you're either promising or you're not.

The "duty to country" is just not going to do much for me. I'm not all that interested in focusing on my duty to my country right now, and it's just not in the moral neighborhood I'm looking at. I mean, I'll vote, and go to PTA meetings and so forth, and maybe someday I'll become civically and politically involved again (though not while a state employee!) but none of that is what I need to be grappling with.

"Helping other people" is obviously a good idea, and having goodwill toward others is part of what I'm looking at here, but again, it's just not really much of a stimulating or useful concept.

The Law of the Pack? Hey, you don't want to know. Oh, you do? Hmmm, I've pretty well forgotten it already, but here is a sort of 50% accurate rendition: "The Cub Scout helps the Pack go, the Pack helps the Cub Scout grow." It's actually a LOT longer than that, two or three times as long, but that will give you the flavor. It's more of a description or program analysis than a law, and it just doesn't make much sense or have much of an impact.

So that's it. Nothing amusing or interesting. It just seems kind of flat to me, not much impact.

I agree completely on the uniforms. As den leader, I wear a khaki shirt with various patches and so forth, and I confess, THOUGH

ONLY TO YOU, that I love wearing it, and do feel different in it. The boys do wear only the shirts and neckerchiefs (marvelous word!) now, but I think even that much is a good experience for them, and they look great. The Girl Scout sweatshirts are no good, I agree. In fact, I have an overall bad impression of Girl Scouting. You sell cookies, do some boring craft projects, and then have huge boring advancement meetings where everyone pretends it's been a valuable learning experience.

I like uniforms too. That's why I insist on wearing my "lawyer uniform." Every day, I wear a very nice suit, pressed shirt, silk tie, etc. My fellow lawyer here agrees. We even discussed it. We dress as lawyers every day. Most government lawyers don't, they end up wearing knit ties, semi-casual pants, corduroy jackets, checked shirts, etc. I don't ever want to become a "government lawyer" (which has implications within the profession), so I will never dress like one. I do believe that what you wear has an impact on who you are, or at least on how you feel and behave. I think school uniforms are a great idea. Also party "uniforms." What you are wearing sort of announces what mode you are operating in, and makes life more interesting.

Man, the knife thing really captured most of my thinking about scouting as a boy. I'm STILL trying to think of a good reason to carry a knife around. Did I buy you one of those compact multi-tools for you? That's sort of the same. I look at them, and I really try hard to think of some reason that I need to buy one and carry it around all the time.

I didn't get the "leaving that aside" reference, but now I just did, and I laughed a lot. That was a pretty nice way to just sort of ease some stuff out of the way, there.

Regarding our relative capacities for "purely creative invention," you're so wrong it hurts. I am pretty creative, but I could cite you chapter and verse at great length to counter your pathetically misguided assessment of our respective gifts in that field. For now, I will only comment that just in the last two weeks you have, apparently without even knowing it, elevated my capacity for thinking in a genuinely creative and innovative way by about 1,000%.

You know what I hate? I hate it when I'm sitting in my office, and I have some really bad gas, and then, in breaking wind, I inject the foul gas into the cushion of my office chair, where it ripens to new heights of putrescence, so that whenever I sit down on the chair for the rest of the day, this invisible cloud of unbelievably vile noxious fumes squirts out, singeing my nose hairs, and visibly startling anyone else who happens to be present.

Is it just me?

* * *

Date: 1/23/96
From: Kevin
Subject: ?

I had the idea to send a message to you, one letter at a time, in the Subject space, like Q U I T F A R T I N G, but I don't think the humor impact would be worth the very minimal effort.

Speaking of farting, I can't believe that I just laughed out loud at your gas-oriented bit. I was already chuckling over the phrase "your pathetically misguided assessment" when you hit me with the great stench scenario, and it caught me just right.

You're right, the Scout Oath and Law sound a little lame, although they may have a different impact on children than they do on adults. "Do my best" could sound like a challenge to a boy, and an escape clause to an adult.

I've wondered about the writer's uniform. It's really too bad that turtlenecks are such an integral part of it, since I like them and think that I look good in them. Having said what I did about uniforms, I feel very reluctant to adopt the style of my trade, probably for the same reason that I've avoided taking writing classes and been cautious about reading authors who are working with themes similar to mine. I don't want to adopt any of the conventions of writing without being aware that I'm doing so.

As for knives and, by extension, tools, they're some of the great things about being an adult. I have my mini Swiss Army knife on my keychain, tools in my glove compartment, more tools in my trunk, and more tools in my garage and toolbox, all of which I use often enough to justify having them. I love it.*

Well, that brings us back around to creativity, something about which we certainly don't need to argue. I know that creativity, like other basic human attributes (such as physical strength, intelligence, and farting) are partly innate and partly the result of development, and it feels wonderful to have re-developed mine during the past year. I'm glad you're feeling it too.

A lasting effect of the 9/11 attacks is the air travel ban on carrying pocket knives, even of keychain size. I realize that, as a practical matter, it's just a small inconvenience, but I hate it, and I hate the terrorists for it.

* * *

Date: 1/24/96
From: Reagan
Subject: Q

I sort of have been puzzled from time to time, in a pleasant way, over the last couple of years, about how pleased I am by that little Swiss Army knife you gave to me, and which I have on my keychain. I do use it quite often, it is handy, but that doesn't seem to be all of it. Now I get it: I finally get to carry a knife around all the time, just as I always wanted to as a child, and not have to feel silly and useless about it. It is handy enough to amply justify its presence in my pocket.

I'm glad you found my "loaded chair" bit amusing. What's tragic is that in addition to being funny, it's a real problem. I'm trying to remember now to stand up before I let one fly, so it doesn't build up in the cushion. I can always tell when I am really eating a healthy diet, because I start having gosh-awful gas and other unpleasant signs of gastrointestinal acceleration. I just laugh when I hear how we should be eating more fiber. When I'm eating healthy, if I just look at fiber, I take off like a rocket. I'd like to get some info on healthy foods that bind you up a bit.

Perhaps there is no real writer's uniform, except to wear clothing that truly suits them. Writing is different from other professions, because it relies almost exclusively on individual creativity. My instincts tell me that your instinct to avoid a writer's uniform is sound. In a way, I think choosing clothes, or interior decor or ANYTHING, on the basis that it is a genuine individual choice is very difficult. It seems all we can do is choose from various packages, and it is hard to avoid making choices to suit others, or for the impact it will have on others, rather than simply making the choice from within.

I know what I don't want. I don't want "country" decor, for example. But is there any merit in choosing some other loosely packaged "look?" Maybe, maybe not. I would like to have a house that truly suits me, but that is very difficult to do, as simple as it sounds. It is hard to avoid adopting other's tastes, wittingly or not. Similarly, when I peruse an LL Bean catalog, it is tempting to say, "I like this look, I'll just buy all my clothes like this." But that seems like a false value, sort of a sucker's choice. I don't want to go around looking like a weirdo, but shouldn't it be possible for me to discern my own truly individual taste in clothing? Or is that an illusion. Maybe fashion and decor are inherently pre-packaged, we should just not waste energy, and just go with a look that seems OK to us.

One thing I sense, is that "non-conformity" is almost always just a different conformity, and often a more rigid conformity. True non-conformity, which I would define as genuine individualism, is either rare or impossible. Is it desirable?

I also like turtlenecks, and like how I look in them, but as I've gotten older my skin has dried out, and now in the winter my skin is dry enough that turtlenecks chafe my skin and are very uncomfortable on my neck. I have a few, but I hardly ever wear them. I may experiment with mock turtlenecks.

***

Date: 1/24/96
From: Reagan
Subject: Is a bonehead

Once again mailed without printing, please boomerang at your convenience.

***

Date: 1/27/96
From: Kevin
Subject: Hey!

Good thoughts on individual style and choice. (Unrelated note: I like the word "thoughty," which I've never heard anyone but you use.)

These relate to the idea of true creativity: the closer you get to it, the less it's like anything else that came before it. This isn't to say that it's not obvious; sometimes creative thinking just involves a realization, looking at something in a way that's never been done before. I think sometimes about the evolving human perception of nature, of things like air and fire and the design and functioning of the body. It's strange to think of myself walking through a field not knowing anything about biology, chemistry, physics, astronomy . . . it would probably be a good feeling, in a way, less noisy inside. I don't bring all that stuff into my consciousness all the time, but it's there at some level, attached to what I'm looking at. It would be more like childhood. Remember sitting in tall grass in a sunny field, not really knowing that much about all the "underlyings" and having what you did know just kind disappear while you experienced the moment? Everything felt more solid and more permanent.

So, where am I here? I was trying to get at the ideas of newness and uniqueness. It's hard to choose something that's not there. Well, wait, it's a lot narrower than that. When we're talking about making lifestyle choices, or about being in a creative profession, we impose a lot of restrictions. Just in clothing styles, it's easy to imagine coming up with stuff that's never been worn before (except on a fashion runway), but most people who want a distinctive look only want one about a degree off from what everyone else is wearing. And in choices about clothing and decor are also the elements of comfort, convenience, and cost (the "Three Cs" of lifestyle choices . . . well, including conformity, that'd be the "Four Cs").

Man, this seemed like it was going to be a lot clearer and simpler when I started. I'm flying off all over the place. Let me re-read what you wrote.

Okay, the important part was knowing what you really want and making a fully individual decision about how you're going to live. The question seems to be: How would you live if you were totally free – if the opinions of others didn't matter, if cost were no object – or would it even matter then? Would it be important to make a fashion statement only to yourself? Would it feel better to wear expensive clothes if money meant nothing? Would comfort become the only criterion?

There's still way too much to cover in a note, and I need to get going to take the girls to tennis.

When I started reading your comment about turtlenecks and your neck, I thought you were going into a Lame Comedy Bit about, you know, having the neck of a turtle, etc. I was ready to chuckle when it turned into a sorry tale of chafing and discomfort, which caused me to be amused anyway because it was so different from what I was expecting. Now, if you did that on purpose, we're talking about REAL creativity!

* * *

Date: 1/29/96
From: Reagan
Subject: Hello again?

If you receive this message, please let me know as soon as possible. I can't print, for some reason, and I'm wondering if I can send.

***

Date: 1/29/96
From: Reagan
Subject: Hello?

This is a test.

***

Date: 1/30/96
From: Kevin
Subject: Hello again!

Yes, I can hear you. Both messages got through.

I've been meaning to mention how often your name comes up in conversation with the girls. They'll frequently comment on how much we're alike: "That sounds like something Uncle Reagan would say," or "That sounds like Uncle Reagan's laugh." Other things will trigger comments too, the most recent being a discussion of songs from Pocahontas. I'm not all that familiar with the songs, but Sarah said that you either liked, or would probably like, a particular one, because it had "meaningful lyrics." They really enjoy having you for an uncle, and seem to have an image of you as being both fun (in the great tradition of fun-loving uncles) and thoughtful.

***

Date: 1/31/96
From: Reagan
Subject: is alert, but jittery

Annie was unwell this morning, so, naturally, I drank her cappuccino too. HEY, I FEEL GOOD!
Too good?

I had a reaction to your latest message similar to the reaction you had to my "chafey turtleneck" message. I got your very kind message about how my nieces like me, and when I was just a little into it, and saw that second sentence ("They'll frequently comment on how much we're alike") I took it for granted that I was getting set up for a punch line involving gaseous emissions. When it didn't come, it was even funnier!

I get the same kind of "uncle comments" from my family, particularly Monica, and particularly since I started wearing contacts, and particularly after I got my hair cut. She'll say, "hey, you look just like Uncle Reagan . . . wait a minute you ARE Reagan, and you're NOT my uncle!" No, actually, I get just about the same comments you related: "You looked/sounded/whatever just like Uncle Kevin when you did that." They all think you're the best! The twins often express the wish that they could show you something they've made or learned. I think they value your opinion and your attentiveness. I also get comments from Annie. Like a few days ago, I had just had my hair cut, so the stage was set. We were sitting and talking, and I burped a little, but contained it in my mouth, thereby puffing out my cheeks a bit, while smiling. She said "Hey, you looked just like Kevin when you did that!" Apparently this confluence of events reproduced something reminiscent of your cheeky smile. This is something you can really feel good about!

The first paragraph of your previous message reminded me of something I've thought about before. Let's suppose you lived thousands of years ago. It would have to be right around the beginning of civilization, when people were in a thinking and learning mode, but hadn't figured much out yet. Let's suppose, for example, that you were walking along, and felt the wind or were watching a bird, and it suddenly hit you that you were surrounded not by nothing but by an invisible substance (air) that is like a thinner form of water. As you said, it's obvious in a way, but it is something that can be discovered and realized, too. What kind of thoughts would you have? Would you wonder if birds can fly to the Moon, and whether you could find a way to make a "boat" that would travel in the air? Would you wonder if air had weight and the other attributes of matter? Just generally speaking, it would be cool to be asking stuff like: "What are the types of matter?" "What is that lightning?" "What is fire?" "Does the earth go on forever?" You could speculate and experiment and come up with all kinds of realizations.

Like dropping balls off a tower, science and discovery used to just require a certain kind of mind, not much equipment.

In a way, knowing what we know does interfere with perception, or with experience. Last summer, I got in the habit of lying in the backyard at night, looking at the stars. I got interested in them, and was about to embark on learning about them, but then thought better of it. I didn't want to turn stargazing into a rational, scientific, analytical, learning experience. I was afraid I wouldn't be able to just look at the stars anymore, I'd have all kinds of thoughts going on.

When you're a kid, you really experience things like seasons, textures, everything, in a direct way. I'm not sure if that's as true as it used to be. Do you remember just lying in the grass, checking out the plants and bugs? Roaming around in the hills, seeing what there was to see. I spent a summer in Minot after law school, and I remembered those little yellow flowers that grew on the bushes in the back (honeysuckle?) that you could pull the middles out of and they were sweet. So I thought I would be sure to do that. But the flowers came and went too quickly. One day I looked, and they weren't "ripe," and then the next time I thought of it, they were drying out. The "season" was like a week or maybe two, but from my childhood memories, it seemed so much longer. I remember sucking some that weren't quite sweet yet, and then getting a bunch of good ones for a while, and then having to hunt for good ones again.

The thing is, we were out there every day, and time seemed so much slower then. I don't know if kids live like that anymore. They don't just hang out outside much, and if they are never bored or at loose ends because of the damn TV. So they never have to discover something, or come up with something, or just hang out and observe things. We keep them penned up and anesthetized.

Remember standing on that metal fence at the Korom's, and spreading out our jackets and jumping into the wind, convinced that we were getting a little bit of "glide" out of it? There is something inherently good about being outside and seeing and handling natural objects. Like fooling around in the snow, making forts and snow people. It is good in itself. I always carry around this mental list of a hundred things I should be doing, so I never get to just "be" anymore. What would it be worth to wake up on a Saturday morning with NOTHING TO DO?

On the other hand, I think I would get more out of trees if I knew more about them. I look at a tree, and there it is. But if you know about trees, you can kind of get more out of it, and see more aspects of it.

This style thing is a tough one. I don't have any interest in looking bizarre, or operating outside the narrow zone of alternatives you mention. So what is true individualism in that context? Impossible? Does it really even have value? Is it worth thinking about? Is a conscious fashion choice ever going to be genuine, or is it inherently artificial? Are consciousness and genuineness mutually exclusive? Is it senseless to think of adopting a fashion that suits only you, to assume that it is wrong to dress for the effect on others, when that is really the only purpose of fashion?

One thing I know: I have more important things to worry about.

Or do I?

The four C's are a classic!

As we discuss this, I am coming to wonder if the concept of living in a totally free and individual way, without regard to the opinions of others, is really a desirable or even meaningful concept. It seems almost inhuman. What is it I'm really after here?

I also like the word "thoughty." It is not my invention. It is a Lee Petersonism. He would say "that was very thoughty of you." The word suited him: mannerly but playful, in a precise way. I believe he enjoyed the "naughtiness" of using a made-up word, a pleasure that is denied to the mass of humanity. I use it sparingly, as I believe even moderate overuse would spoil it, but it is a word I get real pleasure from, particularly since it reminds me of a good friendship.

Gee, I felt bereft without e-mail, even though I only thought I might not have it for a few days. It's great, isn't it?

6. February 1996: Kick the Can

Date: 2/1/96
From: Reagan
Subject: A: "cub jest"

Q: What do you call a prank played by a young boy scout that is also a palindrome for "subject?"

Is that lame or what? I thought I could do something really funny with palindromes for "subject," but that was the best I could do. The only other one was "Jet Bus C," which would have involved some big build up in the context of a 1950's sci-fi book about life in the 1980's. It seemed like a really good idea, but it was just bec. My creativity was a cej bust. Just ask Jeb Scut, he's the best juc-ster I know.

Do I really want to send this to you?

* * *

Date: 2/5/96
From: Kevin
Subject: is alert, but jittery

Ah, yes, caffeine-induced euphoria. I am currently in such a condition and enjoying it mightily. There are apparently many people who naturally feel that way most of the time. Remember how it used to feel to wake up on a sunny summer morning as a kid? Just bounding out of bed, happy and alert and ready to go. Waking up these days feels a lot better than it did during the depression, but I doubt that it will ever have quite the same snap as it did back then.

It occurs to me that this is the second fond look back at childhood that I've come up with recently. It's the result of two things: a desire to balance out the focus on the negative aspects of my past that occurred while working my way to health, and an interest in understanding different modes of thought and ways of perceiving the world.

In reference to the latter, I've recently been going through another phase of reducing my tendency to rely on fantasy, daydreaming and entertainment to satisfy my need for gratification and achievement. I know that that has been a big issue with you at times, and it feels good to be working on it myself. I've begun to realize what tremendous opportunities there are for discovery, experimentation, and fulfillment in "real life." It almost makes another good advertising slogan: "Your life is your movie." I'm just beginning to realize how seductive and addictive this culture of entertainment is. I have it within my power to live a life far more interesting and rewarding than the most fabulous movie. Why? Because I'm capable of experiencing it firsthand, in every detail, writing my own script, dealing with real people doing real things (some of which are truly stranger than fiction), and dealing with surprises, good and bad, that come along. Only I can experience me as fully as I do. As much as I might try to escape, I'm me all the time, and I should enjoy that experience to the fullest.

Speaking of fullest, I'm gratified to know that you've discovered the formula: smiling belch = facsimile of Kevin. I'm sure you'll be able to entertain the girls with this discovery at our next gathering.

Concerning our discussion of the unknowing mind, I am glad (as I assume you are) to be living in this age of knowledge, but I agree that the knowledge can get in the way of direct perception and enjoyment. I like having available as many answers and explanations as currently exist, but I'd also like to re-develop the ability to look at the world with an open mind. In addition to just looking for the sake of enjoyment, I wonder how many things are left to discover that will take little more than a leap of imagination, a flash of recognition.

I do fear for this country, Reag, and the rest of the world too, as it becomes more Westernized. When two of the most popular American television exports of recent years have been Dallas and Baywatch, you know something's wrong. I'm coming to believe more and more that those few who can keep free of the tentacles of the culture, particularly the media, who can connect without being controlled, will be the only ones with a real chance to direct their lives and destinies. I'm sure you've noticed the incursion of television into public places like restaurants, airline terminals, waiting rooms – it's like a science fiction movie, where the populace seems unaware of the creeping menace while we watch in dismay. Great, huh? We finally get rid of smoking as a public nuisance and along comes another form of pollution to take its place.

I borrowed a little from Monty Python's Spanish Inquisition sketch for the Four Cs bit. In fact, the girls stayed here last night and I rented a Best Of video which included the Spanish Inquisition. We were dismayed to find that, with the exception of that part, the stuff ranged from mildly entertaining to boring. I began fast-forwarding, and we all agreed that it was a little funnier that way. Sarah had a great line: "It's humor without the commitment."

So, does this make sense? I rail on about TV and then rent a video to watch with the girls. Yeah, I'm ambivalent, and I'll admit that there's some good stuff to watch. It seems like the situation you described with campaign spending: no one could figure out how to best spend money, only that the more you spent the more likely you were to win. With TV, it's easy to make the argument that some of what's on is educational, or informative, or quality entertainment, but it just seems that the more people watch TV, the worse off they and society will be.

Yes, I really like e-mail. It's helped me to keep in close contact with you, and has provided a way of communicating with you that is much better than paper mail and better in some ways than the telephone. I like having a printed record of our "conversations," and I like having time to stop and think about things as I'm writing.

I laugh every time I read your "subject" message. It took me back to Boys' Life – did we ever read Boys' Life? Well, stuff like that, anyway, with anagrams and rebuses, jokes, and riddles. Were they ever really funny? As I recall, it was mostly a matter of how lame the answer or punch line would be.

Q: How many elephant tusks does it take to make a piano keyboard?

A: Who cares? Hunting elephants is fun!

I'm looking at the Life Nature Library volume on Africa, copyright 1964. Here are a couple of photo captions:

> Grinning broadly, movie cowboy Roy Rogers poses with, from left to right, a kudu, a porcupine, an eland, a lesser sable antelope, a warthog and a waterbuck, part of his bag on a 1962 safari in Mozambique. Object of the three-week-long hunt was not big game but rare antelope, the skins of which were sent home for mounting as trophies. The safari, on which Rogers and another client were accompanied by two white hunters, included two Land Rovers, 25 natives, and a refrigerator.

> Hunter of the new school, Arthur Godfrey disembarks from a helicopter used to spot game and herd it toward rifles – and to shorten an elephant kill from a week to two hours.

Now, that's huntin', eh, fellas?

Oh, by the way, I've found that I can save considerable time on Prodigy by writing my messages in WordPerfect, storing them in the proper format, and calling them up and sending them in Prodigy. I think you asked about that a while back, and it does work.

* * *

Date: 2/6/96
From: Reagan
Subject: is inspired by your message

I have been getting away from that reality-instead-of-fantasy thing lately, much to my regret. I am getting that nagging feeling that there are all kinds of things I should be thinking about, but don't seem to have time to. I need to even out here, get back to that "living my life" feeling. I am glad to hear you are doing it. Part of it, I think, is just that I have been sick off and on for several weeks, and that I've gotten into a pattern of not getting enough sleep.

Those photo captions were remarkable. It's amazing how quickly values and perceptions can change. The idea that the rarity of the antelopes made it more desirable to kill them, or that it was good to come up with a quicker way to find and shoot elephants. Also dismaying that the natives ranked between the Land Rovers and refrigerator in importance, and that they were on the "gear list" rather than the "other humans" list.

Similar to your Python experience, several years ago Annie and I rented Woody Allen's "Everything You Ever Wanted to Know About Sex" and it wasn't funny at all, which was disturbing, because we remembered really enjoying it in college. I hope "The Holy Grail" is still funny, and "Life of Brian."

People talk about how great Woody Allen's early movies are, but I don't like them much. However, everything from "Annie Hall" onward I like a lot. His movies seem handmade. I rent them, and watch them alone, mostly, although I watched "Manhattan Murder Mystery" with Annie, and I actually think it made that one better.

Regarding memories of childhood and sunny days: We were playing kick the can. I think I was in my early grade school years, maybe six or seven years old. The can was in our back yard. I had adopted the high-risk strategy of hiding beside our side door, on the east side of the entryway. The idea was, when the person who was "it" would come up along the side driveway, you would have to be ready to jump out and run, and to time it just right to try to get the drop on him, so that even though he was starting closer to the can, you could maybe beat him back to the can. If he saw you before you bolted out, he would be closer to the can plus have the drop, and you would be sunk. It was more of an ambush location than a hiding spot.

There was no planter wall then. I was tucked back into the corner. I could hear the "it" person coming slowly up the drive. Obviously he was aware that someone might be hiding where I was, and was primed for it. My chance of success was small. I was trying to calculate the angle at which I would become visible to him, so I could jump out just before he got to that point, and, of course I was trying to scrunch myself back as much as possible, while also being ready to jump out and run.

There was exceptionally bright sunlight. It must have been mid-afternoon, as the sunlight created a shadow forming a right triangle, with the wall of the house and the wall of the side entry forming the right angle, and the line of the shadow forming the 45-degree angle across. I knew that sunlight was in the form of rays or beams that struck objects, and then were reflected back into viewer's eyes. I made a conceptual error. I confused the angle the sunlight was coming from (from the sun) with the angle it would travel back to the "it" person's eyes. So I reached a false conclusion, momentarily, that as long as no part of me extended from the shadow into the sunlight, I would be OK. I think I was a little bewildered by the conclusion (I didn't actually think I was invisible in the shadow, I was just thinking about angles) but it seemed logical, so I stopped scrunching so hard against the wall and got into a "ready to run" position, with none of me extending into the sunlight.

Of course, the person who was "it" edged forward and peered at me from about ten feet away and then took off for the can. I was caught completely flat footed. My error sank in. Obviously, even though I was in the shadow, at some point the "it" person would come to a point where he could just look over and see me.

I didn't actually feel very bad about it, maybe a little chagrined. Looking back on it, I'm still pretty satisfied with the thought processes I went through. I think it was a sophisticated series of ideas to have had at that age, even though they led to a boneheaded mistake on that occasion. I think the brightness of the sunlight had something to do with it. The contrast between light and dark was so strong, that you could really focus on the line of the shadow.

So there is a childhood memory for you!

* * *

Date: 2/7/96
From: Kevin
Subject: +

Yep, amazing how easy it is to get thrown off track, often without noticing it. Getting sick almost always does it, and sleep deprivation is no help. And having THE NECK OF A TURTLE . . . well, say no more.

You certainly have a way with words – "gear list" vs. "other humans list." Sums it up, all right.

I have yet to see many of Woody Allen's later movies. I recall liking "Annie Hall" when it came out, but I haven't seen it since. I enjoyed "The Purple Rose of Cairo" when it first came out and again when I rented it a few weeks ago. I saw "Manhattan Murder Mystery" in the theater and was entertained but not all that impressed. What are your favorites? What do you like in a girl? Are you a party guy or do you prefer quiet evenings at home? Do fruits and vegetables figure prominently in your daily diet? In your pants? Do murmuring voices in your head tell you to disregard the shrill, demanding voices in your head? Are great masses of fur-like hair beginning to cover your butt? When you get nervous, do you find yourself smoothing down your eyebrows with your tongue? How much snow does it take to cover an imaginary animal? Can you melt aluminum pans with concentrated beams of energy flashing out from your eyes?

Should cheese really be considered a food? How can I stop this bit, with the shrill, demanding voices in my head urging me on?

Great stuff on childhood memory. I have many similar memories of our games: kick the can, spotnik*, broom hockey, round-the-block races, Batman, army, cushion fights**, freeze tag . . . bet you were expecting more wacky comedy, huh? Nope, not here, pal.

*A version of tag, played in the autumn when it got dark early, in which the person who was "it" would tag people with the beam of a flashlight.

**We'd whack each other with old couch cushions, which sounds innocuous enough except that they were full of steel springs and could deliver quite a blow. We would frequently knock each other to the ground.

* * *

Date: 2/8/96
From: Kevin
Subject: -

I found a short piece you wrote some years back about winter in North Dakota, and e-mailed it to Deborah's mom. Here it is:

> Those who have not lived in the northern plains of North America, or in some equally cold region, if there is one, may not appreciate the fine nuances of winter temperatures, but they are important to those of us who, by choice or by chance, live in the harsh climate of this region. For us, cold winter weather comes in several varieties, most of them unobjectionable, and some even pleasant. A sunny winter day in the high twenties is sloppy but fun, perfect for snowmen, snowforts, and snowball fights, lousy for ice-skating on a mushy outdoor rink. If it is after December it constitutes a heat wave, and everyone will be out in sweaters or jackets, shoveling their driveways, or doing their shopping, pretending spring is going to come early this year, and stay.

February 1996: Kick the Can

The high teens and low twenties are the best for real winter fun. Step outside into twenty degrees, and you are transformed by the bracing cold against your face and the deliciously cool air expanding your lungs. You feel immediately more awake, and filled with a vigorous energy, as though the cold air had twice its normal oxygen content. You smile a broad smile, and your mood shifts to one of hearty goodwill toward the world and your fellow humans. Here is a day for doing good things. If only there were some wonderful old-fashioned thing to do, like a sleigh ride with singing, or a big evergreen to be toppled to serve as the Christmas tree on Main Street. As fine substitutes, parents and children go sledding, ambitious types cross-country ski, and everyone does an extra good job shoveling the sidewalk in front of the yard, clearing the cement right to the edge, with a beautiful crisp border revealing just a few green blades of the snugly buried grass.

As a teenager, my friends and I, inspired by the wholesome energy imparted by cold air, would roam the city at night when blizzards struck, looking for motorists stuck in snowdrifts, just so we could exercise our newly-strong muscles in pushing them free. A rare and precious combination of adolescent nighttime excitement and neighborly benevolence.

Temperatures between zero and fifteen are the bread and butter of winter life on the northern plains. Not cold enough to complain about at the office, nor warm enough to inspire spontaneous outdoor fun, just climate as usual during the short winter days. Drive to work in the dark, drive home in the dark, try not to start wishing for spring too soon, or else the cabin fever will get mighty bad come March, when our ancient internal clocks expect warm breezes, but our geographic location inexorably delivers another solid month of winter.

Below zero, the outdoor world becomes an alien and inhospitable environment. Two weeks in January with the thermometer never climbing above zero and everyone becomes withdrawn and short-tempered. Children cooped up in their houses become simultaneously listless and manic, pushing their edgy parents into barking reprimands and hasty spankings. Step outside in twenty below. You have one short moment of grace in the outside air in which you can begin to pretend that it is not that cold after all, and then your breath burns in your lungs and the slightest shift in position brings the suddenly frigid cloth of your pants unbearably against the skin of your legs.

Forty degrees below zero does not feel much colder than twenty below. In fact, anything below zero feels about equally cold. This is not to say that these temperatures feel the same, it is just that whatever yardstick the human nervous system has for distinguishing the quality "coldness" apparently ends around zero degrees Fahrenheit, and so as the weather drops below that temperature, the difference is perceived according to a different quality: that of bitterness. Zero is cold, twenty below is bitter, forty below is inhumanly bitter.

* * *

Date: 2/8/96
From: Kevin
Subject: caution

I thought you should see part of a message that Deborah's mom sent to me.

> I got a message from a friend this a.m. warning me about a new very destructive virus that comes through the internet e-mail. Can ruin your hard drive. It has as Subject the words "Good Times." And is let into your system if you "read" it. I was advised to let anyone with whom I corresponded know about this. Thus this warning. I haven't been able to find out if this is legit, but I suspect it is. The message he forwarded was very official looking and he is not known for practical jokes. Have you ever seen this kind of thing before? I still have the original message from my friend and can let you see it if you want. Let me know.

Even if this particular warning is a hoax, it's worth considering the possibility of a virus coming through e-mail. For some reason, I hadn't thought about it at all.

I'm going to be mailing out Valentines before I leave tomorrow. When they arrive, you may notice that you didn't get one. This is because card design is apparently going the way of good comic strips. If you want one with a picture of Cupid sticking out his ass at a dismayed couple, I'll send you one next year.

* * *

Date: 2/12/96
From: Reagan
Subject: My new address

I joined AOL last night. My internet email address at home is "pufall@aol.com."

Apparently I am the first Pufall in America to join AOL! If for some reason you ever decide to switch, I will be happy to become rpufall, which I may do anyway.

Please try sending a message to me at home when you get back. I will send a test message to you from home in the meantime. If all goes well, I want to switch most of my emailing to my home.

More later.

* * *

Date: 2/12/96
From: Reagan
Subject: tanks for the memories

I am in the middle of the fifth volume of Churchill's history of World War II. It has been fascinating. He tells the story from his own perspective, and structures the story around his own memos to various people written at the time, which actually form the core of the narrative. He seems to have conducted the war in large part through dictated memos, so you really get the on-the-spot view.

He recounts the military aspect of the war mainly in outline, although he does from time to time present a more detailed account of a particular battle in greater detail. He alternates between the military story in the field and the political story at home and in relation to other countries such as the US, the USSR, the empire dominions, etc. He also throws in personal details, which are sometimes amusing in a very understated way.

There are many aspects of this that I would like to share with you. It has been informative and thought provoking. Anyway, between the book and a recent magazine article, I got some old history and fresh perspective on tanks, which, as you may recall, are a pet topic of mine from college. Turns out the British invented tanks (or so says Churchill) but then did not effectively develop them either in design or tactics, while the Germans did both. The British tanks were grossly undergunned, they really had pathetic little guns. The British did not seem to have focused on the tank's cannon as being the key thing.

The British suffered an uninterrupted string of horrible military disasters from the end of 1941 to the last part of 1943. Amazing setbacks and failures. In one sphere, Rommel had marched the British east across the North coast of Africa, and was poised to take Cairo, the Nile, Egypt, and the Suez Canal, which would have been a gigantic disaster for reasons both obvious and subtle. Anyway, two things then happened: first, the British yanked General Auchinleck and put in Generals Alexander and Montgomery; and second, several hundred American Sherman tanks and 105 mm anti-tank mobile guns arrived. Also, Rommel was overextended. Anyway, the British then kicked Rommel's butt big time and just chased him at an amazing pace all the way back across Africa. For the British, that was the turning point of their fortunes.

What I thought you would be really interested in, though, was the new stuff I read in a magazine. Take what follows as maybe 75% accurate. As you may know, shaped charges were for many years the main anti-tank weapon. The bazooka was an early example. The rounds that tanks shot at each other also followed this design. The idea was that when the shell hits the tank's armor, it explodes forward, injecting molten and incendiary material into the tank. The big delivery system for this eventually was guided missiles, like TOW missiles (wire guided) and remote or smart cruise type missiles.

Two defenses emerged. First, active armor, in which there are explosives on the outside of the tank. When the missile hits, the charge on the armor literally "blows it away." Since the missile costs a LOT more than the charges (maybe more than the tank!) this is not a good balance for the attacker, even if the charge defense is not foolproof. Second, the British developed Chobham armor, which is a layered armor, alternating steel with a substance that has apparently been successfully kept secret, maybe ceramic or some composite. Anyway, the layers successfully resist and redirect the shaped charge, so the ignited gases or molten substance doesn't penetrate through the layers. Chobham armor can only be produced in flat sheets, which is why the M1 (which uses it) looks so slab-sided.

Then came the armor piercing shells, in which a finned needle of depleted uranium is fired at high speed via a sabot out of a tank or anti-tank cannon. These punch through Chobham. I learned that the needles do not just shatter and ricochet inside, but that the surface of the uranium, heated by contact with the armor, ignites and fills the tank with very high temperature combusting metal, setting off whatever is in there, which generally leads the tank to blow up real good. Pictures of Iraqi tanks from desert storm show them with the whole top half pretty well blown off or apart.

So now apparently the US is making a new version of the layered armor for the M1A1 and the new M1A2 in which some of the layers are depleted uranium! There are stories of M1A1 tanks driving around with Iraqi (Soviet) needle-type projectiles sticking out of them, like arrows out of a covered wagon!

I just had to share this with you.

* * *

Date: 2/18/96
From: Kevin
Subject: We're back!*

Hi dad,
We just got back from Florida. Everything was fun except for the trip in the car. I will be leaving tomorrow, but I don't know what time. I had lots of fun in Disney World! I got everybodies autograph except for Launchpads. Guess what? The whole time I was there I never saw Mickey! You guys didn't send a present for Uncle Fuzzy's birthday. Hopefully it is in the mail! I'm so happy you joined America on Line! Upon my return you will have to show me how to use it. See ya soon!
   Your Loving, and tan daughter,
   Monica

Monica, emailing Reagan from my house upon returning from our trip to Disney World.

* * *

Date: 2/19/96
From: Reagan
Subject: to further testing

This is only a test. This is a test of the Pufall e-mail system. In the event of a real e-mail, you would be reading something amusing. But this is only a test.

Monica got back safely, but she must have caused some trouble on the flight, because they brought her off the plane in leg irons. She said she had a lot of fun in Florida, "except for my relatives being around, of course."

She is standing behind me hitting me in the head. It hurts. This part is really true.

Now it's her turn:

Hello Uncle Fuzzy,

Has the IRS arrested you yet for secretly sending messages to China through a transmitter in your stomach? When they do I will overflow with joy!

Your loving and caring niece,

Monica (if this were my real signature it would be a lot more interesting)

Thank you for getting Monica back here safely. One nice thing about the way this trip went, nothing much is going to bother her when she travels in the future!

Just in case you were wondering, no, I have not mailed your present to you yet. I have, however, thought about doing so a lot this week, and it's the thought that counts, in some strange alternate universe in which real accomplishment is irrelevant.

You will have to tell me how to do that thing where you type a message on the word processor and then attach it and mail it on the net. I can just feel the money flowing out through the wires as I type, and it is not a sensation conducive to relaxed creativity.

Sabrina's turn:

Hi! This is Sabrina so how is it doing up there? Did you like disney world? I can hardly wait for our next visit!

Reagan D's turn:

Hi uncle Kevin how's itsgoing.I have a new mexican pupit. Its hard to move.see you later.

Annie's in bed, so that's it for the northern Pufalls.

* * *

Date: 2/22/96
From: Kevin
Subject: This 'n' that

Had another music-related idea: what would the soundtrack of your life include? What songs would you pick for a movie version of your life? I haven't gone any farther than that myself, it just sounded like an interesting idea.

So, yes, your test worked. I got the message without being even slightly amused. I look forward to many such messages in the future. Mighty pleased with that prospect.

Message to Monica: "Back! Back, foul creature, to the fetid depths whence you sprang!" No, wait, that message was for the hideous, reptilian monster which is gnawing on my leg. My message for Monica is: "Back! Back, hideous reptilian monster . . ." Okay, okay, really, here's the message: I'm really glad you could come on the trip, it was great fun having you along. The pictures I took turned out nicely, and I'm sending a bunch of copies to you today. Be sure to share them with your family. Thanks for being so cooperative on the trip back. It was a long drive in a cramped car, and you endured it with great patience.

Here's what I do to avoid being in Mail too long. I type the message in my word processing program (WordPerfect). When I do Save As under File, there is a line marked Format. In Format are a number of options, of which I choose ASCII (DOS) Text. There is a brief conversion process, and the file is saved (under whatever filename I choose). Then I start Prodigy Mail, in which there is an option to import text. I just type in the filename and up scrolls my message! Let me know if this works with your setup. (I just did this, and realized that the suffix of the filename can make a difference. I can't call up files with .wpd on the end, but .txt will work.)

Message for Sabrina: "Back! Back, lovely birdlike creature . . ." No, that just doesn't work at all, does it? Anyway, yes, I did like Disney World. I know that you'll like it when you go there with your family, and I hope I'm along when you do. I'm sure we'll be up to visit you this spring, which is right around the corner.

Message for Reag (no fooling around, this time): Hey, it's going great. Thanks for asking. Was the puppet a gift from Monica? She had a lot of fun shopping for everyone while she was on her trip. I hope the puppet gets easier to use as you practice.

Message for Annie: ZZZZZZZZ. (Which is, of course, not to suggest that you snore. I'm just trying to set the mood for blissful slumber.)

So, would you rather get e-mail at work or at home? Or does it matter? Please advise.

Thanks for the tank stuff. I'm a sucker for military hardware and, to a somewhat lesser extent, military history. I can't say that I know a lot about either, but I do enjoy books and articles about them. I'm sure I'd enjoy the Churchill history that you're reading. I'll add it to my list.

Oh, here you said you want to "switch most of my emailing to my home." Well, too bad, bub. You're getting this one at work.

* * *

Date: 2/28/96
From: Reagan
Subject: You are dropping stones into a well

Kev, will you, for now, go back to sending email to my work address? I haven't logged onto email at home in about a week, and until I do some reorganizing and so forth, it's going to be a hit and miss for me at home. So until further notice, please resume the old address. I am really feeling the need to communicate with you regularly.

* * *

Date: 2/28/96
From: Kevin
Subject: You are dropping stones into a well

Well, no stones dropped from here. I haven't felt that I've had much to say, although my life is plenty dynamic these days. I got it into my head to write a short sex article of the variety that you see in all the women's magazines in the grocery store. Basically, it was one of those "Hey, I could do that!" moments, and I was over half done with it that same day. I decided that I needed some quotes on the topic (which I won't specify here), since all the articles appear to have them, so I interviewed four female acquaintances, who were pleasantly open with their thoughts. I finished transcribing the tapes and notes today, and should get the thing in the mail tomorrow. Then, back to the self-help book.

Got a call from Mom last night, and she sounded mighty energetic. She says the hot tub has been a great help physically. And she's running for office again!* No moss grows on that gal. Hey, maybe we could produce some attack ads for her. In fact, we wouldn't even have to know who they were. We'd just have a stern/oily-voiced announcer saying: "The foes of Sally Pufall . . . and you know who you are, you kowtowing stamp collectors . . . should be killed, if that is what they deserve. Their views are out of alignment with yours, the great listening public. They are an irritant, an unnecessary risk. Sally Pufall is not one of them. She should be your choice. You must shun all others. Thank you."

Our mother, Sally (Rich) Pufall, served two terms as a County Commissioner in Ward County, North Dakota. She also taught at the collegiate level, was area director for Lutheran Social Services, and established a private counseling practice. And she is a wonderful mom.

* * *

Date: 2/29/96
From: Kevin
Subject: Slime

Hey, this is easy!

"The foes of Sally Pufall are many, and they are not to be trusted. There is a strange odor about them. They have their hands in many pockets. You would do well to see that they are eliminated. Sally Pufall is the one to stand up to her foes, to tell them that they are not wanted. Do not vote for her foes. That is just what they want. They will call you on your telephone. They will rap on the door of your house. Do not listen to their throaty whining. Vote for Sally Pufall, and let her foes slink back into the shadows."

I could get a link of knockwurst elected to office!

7. March 1996: Somewhere in the Center of My Torso

Date: 3/1/96
From: Kevin
Subject: ^ :)

The subject is "Happy Guy Tipping his Thinking Cap." You know what? I don't like the rule concerning punctuation and quotes at the end of a sentence. Like, in the first sentence of this paragraph, the rule says that the quotes should go on the outside of the period. But the period isn't part of the quote! If I had ended the sentence with a question mark or an exclamation point, it would make even less sense to have them inside the quotes. Well, that's all I have to say on that right now.

Obviously, this message is neither urgent nor in need of a receipt. I just thought I'd see if checking those boxes made any difference on your end. Did they? Or am I just confusing you? Come to think of it, you've always had a strange odor about you. I'm beginning to wonder if you are skulking foe.

Okay, you're not a skulking foe. I just tried sending this message, and got a Helpful Prompt informing me that neither the Urgent nor Receipt properties are supported for Internet recipients. Wow, cool feature.

***

Date: 3/4/96
From: Kevin
Subject: DO-IT-URSELF HUMOR PIECE

All parts included

Assembly required

Tools needed: Parody schtick, cliche drill, nonsense-o-meter

Instructions: Make it funny

THE PIECES

1. Mourning the loss of "Keyless" Chuck Nordstrom, memorable member of Nodak ball clubs in the mid-to-late Fifties.

    A. Fan favorite

    B. Brief stint as celebrity spokesman for St. Paul brewery

    C. Played all positions during four-year career, including one disastrous inning as pitcher

2. Reminiscences from past associates.

    A. Carl Lundberg, manager of Fargo Fahrenheits during Chuck's half-season stint: "Who? No, I don't . . . oh, THAT guy. Oh, well . . . dead, huh? What from? Shame. Any family? Well, too bad. Hope he went quick."

    B. Ron White, roommate during much of '57 season: "Oh . . . well, too bad. Did he leave anything for me? Ha ha. He owed me $150 for motel damages. That was a lot of money back then."

    C. Betty Nordstrom Callahan (ex-wife): "What? I thought he . . . well, he must have recovered. Are you a lawyer or something? I am NOT responsible for his bills."

3. Sly reference to the level of his play, mixed with deft inferences as to his intelligence and athletic ability.

A. Patented "flop-catch"

B. Unique "wristless" throwing style

C. "Bullfighter" batting stance

D. "Dumb as a post. And we're talking a real low-level post."

4. Humorous retelling of the origins of his nickname (lost in a blind drunk, robbed & beaten, rolled by grifters, etc.)

Ron White: "Yeah, he was always losing his motel keys, I threatened to staple one to his ass the next time he woke me at 3 a.m. pounding on the door. He actually came back once with the key IN his ass, and I had to go find a doctor, because back then the motel keys were attached to big plastic tags."

5. His astonishingly poor record in the minors and unfortunate attempt to extort his way into the majors.

6. End of career, jail time, divorce, etc.

7. Pathetic comeback attempt.

8. Drift into obscurity.

* * *

Date: 3/7/96
From: Reagan
Subject: is in a burned out haze

Four messages! My little red mailbox runneth over.

I got "Well, well, well," "Slime," "DO-IT-URSELF," and "^ :)" at work. I got "Slime" at home.

Note the punctuation.

March 1996: Somewhere in the Center of My Torso

I am burning the candle on more ends than I thought I had, and yet I am living a mediocre life in a relatively ineffective manner. How do really dynamic, successful people do it?

The attack ads were great. You certainly found a unique "voice" there. I particularly like the "throaty whining." I wonder what would happen if you really ran ads like that? What would happen if a candidate just stepped over some line and ran a deliberately theatrical campaign? Not any lies or anything, but just a distinctly overblown and non-fact based approach. In fact, you wouldn't even mention your opponent or anything about him, or address any other specific real issues. Just elliptical but really dramatic stuff like your messages. Go over the top. "Only Smith can save our society from collapse." "Smith's outstanding background and experiences make him the only candidate qualified to overcome our serious problems." A campaign devoid of any promises or statements of fact. A campaign that could only be viewed as a performance of some kind. The underlying message would be that the modern media public knows all the campaign stuff is just bullshit anyway, so here's one that at least is honest enough to openly be an act.

It could work!

The Nordstrom piece was funny, but also poignant. I particularly liked the "'wristless' throwing style."

"I tried skulking once, but I just didn't know what I was skulking fo'."

AOL, as far as I can tell, offers nothing of interest to me in its own universe.* I am going to try venturing into the WWW itself soon. That's right, I'm becoming a professional wrestler!

I've heard of bargain web connection services with unlimited line time, without universes of their own. I think I may go that route, once I learn more about it.

*AOL was attempting to create its own self-contained, curated subset of the internet. The expectation was that its users would spend all *their online time within that bubble rather than venturing unguided into the world wide web as a whole. It seems like a strange notion now, but it wasn't obviously wrong at the time. Everyone was trying to see into the online future, inevitably with mixed results.*

* * *

Date: 3/11/96
From: Kevin
Subject: You. Let's talk about you for a while.

Actually, all I wanted to do was to remind you to send Monica's airline ticket to me (including folder, receipts, etc.) if you still have it. Thanks!

* * *

Date: 3/12/96
From: Kevin
Subject: Book proposal

I just mailed a preliminary book proposal for my depression self-help book. I would be very interested in hearing your comments and suggestions for changes, deletions, additions, clarifications, etc.

Thanks for letting me look through your own self-help writings in gathering information for my book, and thanks to you and Annie for years of help and insight that enabled me to get healthy and which form an important part of this book.

* * *

Date: 3/13/96
From: Reagan
Subject: Just some quotes

> There is only one success: to be able to spend your life in your own way.
>
> Christopher Morley

> I displayed the smiling countenance and confident air which are thought suitable when things are very bad.
>
> Winston Churchill
> Their Finest Hour

* * *

Date: 3/15/96
From: Kevin
Subject: Just one quote

"What th' . . . !"

Lunkheaded super-villain

* * *

Date: 3/21/96
From: Kevin
Subject: Phone message

For some reason, I've felt more like calling than e-mailing lately. Anyway, I got back into nutritional supplements a few weeks ago, and have noticed a decreased desire for caffeine, as well as an increased sensitivity to it. I would say that over the past couple of years, I've become a light, regular user of caffeine, either in coffee or pop (there's a real regionalism, eh?), so I have some knowledge of my body's tolerance for it and reaction to it. It may be a coincidental and transitory condition, but I know that caffeine has played a role in your life recently, and I thought that you might be interested in alternatives.

* * *

Date: 3/25/96
From: Kevin
Subject: Nothing exciting

I've been busy, but not in ways that make for good e-mail. On one hand, I've been doing a fair amount of mental gymnastics, looking around in my head for new stuff, but it's too amorphous to put into words. On the other hand, I've started working for Mick, who has a floor-cleaning business. Needless to say, the work I'm doing for him is considerably different from what I've become accustomed to.

Somewhere in the center of my torso (having run out of hands), I continue to work on the self-help book. I haven't heard from the agent on either book for a while, so I'm feeling a bit unfocused right now. I don't want to spend too much time working in a direction that could end up changing.

* * *

Date: 3/27/96
From: Kevin
Subject: You

It has come to my attention that it's about time that we got together. Let's come up with a plan.

* * *

Date: 3/28/96
From: Kevin
Subject: Book

I'm reading "KGB: The Inside Story," by a British writer and a KGB defector. Very interesting stuff so far, although there are so many names and so much activity that it's like a very complicated movie. I just have to read on without trying to remember who's who all the time.

It's giving me more of a feeling for why some people did what they did, particularly the Western spies, many of whom were apparently duped into picturing themselves as working for the world-wide Communist movement rather than for Soviet intelligence (at least

March 1996: Somewhere in the Center of My Torso

during the earlier years). It's also amazing to see how non-spying sympathizers (with assistance from the Soviets) basically blinded themselves to the tremendous horrors of Stalin's collectivization program.

> After a tour of Potemkin villages, Bernard Shaw announced: "I did not see a single under-nourished person in Russia, young or old. Were they padded? Were their hollow cheeks distended by pieces of India rubber inside?"

Cleverness can sure come back around and bite your ass.

I'm up to the middle of WWII, the beginnings of which were a real low point for Soviet intelligence. Its ranks had been decimated by Stalin, and even though those who survived had still managed to warn him repeatedly about and impending Nazi invasion, he refused to believe it, and did not even authorize resistance until some hours after the invasion began. It turns out that our pal Churchill had also warned him, but, of course, Stalin had treated the information as part of a ruse.

I think I'd like to read a biography of Stalin. The term "head case" keeps coming to mind as I read about him in this book. Even given the pressures of running a circus like the Soviet Union of the Thirties, it's hard to understand how he could have done what he did. With my limited knowledge, it seems possible to imagine a much different personality being in his position at that time and steering the country down a much more successful path. Here's part of a directive for the elimination of opposition in Lithuania:

> Active abolition of the leading influence of parties hostile to the State: Nationalists, Voldemarists, Populists, Christian Democrats, Young Lithuanians, Trotskyists, Social Democrats, National Guardsmen and others.

Oh, those Voldemarists! Those sly devils! Yes, I think that history has certainly shown Stalin's foresight in eliminating that threat.

Is it just a problem with translation, or do all Crazy Foreign Political Types speak and write in the same stilted manner? There seems to be a style common to anti-Western groups.

> Now that it has been demonstrated that Trotskyist-Zinovievite monsters are uniting in a struggle against Soviet power all the most embittered and sworn enemies of the toilers of our country – spies, provocateurs, saboteurs, White Guards, kulaks, etc.; now that all distinctions have been erased between these elements on the one hand and the Trotskyists and Zinovievites on the other – all our Party organizations, all members of the Party, must understand that the vigilance of Communists is required in any sector and in every situation. The inalienable quality of every Bolshevik in current conditions must be to know how to discover an enemy of the Party, however well he is disguised."

It's interesting that the lack of Japanese activity in the Soviet East enabled the Soviets to make military transfers to the German East. There was apparently a fair amount of debate in Japan as to whether to attack the Soviet Union or Britain and the U.S. Interesting to speculate on the outcome of the war if the decision had gone the other way.

* * *

Date: 3/30/96
From: Reagan
Subject: My whiny excuses

Sorry for the dearth of communication coming back from me to you. I have had severe computer woes at work, and on those few occasions when I have had time to respond to your messages, my system either locked up or shut down.

I have now just done the computer relocation in my home that I mentioned to you. It's now up in the study, which is sort of my room. Anyway, if everything works out as I envision, I will be logging on to AOL every day or two. Please send messages to my home from here on out, and let's see if we can reestablish a good communication flow.

It's 12:30 am, and I've been moving furniture for several hours, so that will have to do it for now. Thanks for the messages! I have enjoyed them and will try to respond soon.

* * *

Date: 3/31/96
From: Reagan
Subject: Goading usefully

I'm sitting here with Annie and she is observing the creation and sending of an authentic e-mail message.

Anything you'd like to say Annie?

No.

She's either intrigued or unimpressed.
Let's trade our WWII books at some point.

In response to one of your messages to my at-work address, yes, let's go ahead and start making some plans to get together soon. Also, I now have a shotgun on layaway, so next fall I will have two (count 'em two) shotguns. That translates into one for each of us. I am at this time wrestling with the demons who tempt me to sip from the cup of dog ownership. It is certainly quite an appealing thought: you and me roaming the moors, watching an eager young pup scourge the bracken for our prey. Based on my scanty experience to date, watching the dog is actually about half the fun.

On a more short-term basis, you and yours are certainly welcome here. We now have a bed surplus to the tune of four, so there is ample room, and an actual (sort of) guest room. I've been sort of assuming we will come down again for the fourth, so let me know how that might be looking this year. We'd better start looking for cannon fuse!*

*Each year Kevin and I would create a fireworks "grand finale" for the entertainment of our children. For our first effort, we built a two-tiered stand out of scrap wood, glued various fireworks to it, and draped strips of T-shirt material soaked with lighter fluid across the fuses. Not surprisingly, the whole thing quickly turned into a raging conflagration, with sparks and shots flying haphazardly out of the flames. It wasn't the effect we were after – and it was over more quickly than we had envisioned – but it was kind of fabulous in its own way and the kids loved it. Each year we refined our methods. A major breakthrough was when Kevin discovered we could purchase lengths of "cannon fuse" – the thick green type used on larger fireworks – to ignite each firework piece in sequence. Eventually, the shows were extensive, multi-platform extravaganzas.

8. April 1996: Truth du Jour

Date: 4/2/96
From: Reagan
Subject: Stop the world!

I need to find a time and a way to absorb and catch up on what has happened in my life. I drove to Fargo today to give a speech. I drove a state car. Early morning start, scrambling, kind of a crazy day, missed some connections. I showed up just in time, and gave a speech to a pretty big crowd, maybe 100 or 150 people, on a controversial workers comp ballot measure. Then I visited some of the lawyers at my old firm who are now working for me. After that, I thought I would cruise through the old neighborhood.

So I'm driving past the house we recently lived in, going down a street I drove at least twice a day for three years which is filled with memories of the kids, in a car I don't own, after giving this big speech and visiting my old firm where I no longer work, plus I'd been up until 2:00 a.m. last night working on my new task force thing*, and suddenly I am just completely disoriented. I have felt like I've been playing catch up with the events in my life ever since college, but this is just too much. I really need to build reflective "alone with myself" time into my daily life.

*I had proposed the creation of a task force aimed at redesigning and improving the claims operation. It was approved and – to my great surprise – I was put in charge of it. The success of that task force was one reason that a few months later I was – to my even greater surprise – promoted to Chief Operating Officer. That was my managerial growth curve: overnight I went from being a lawyer with no supervisory duties to an executive running about half the company. It was, as they say, an opportunity rich environment.

* * *

Date: 4/3/96
From: Reagan
Subject: RE: You

Starting with the assumption that we will be coming down again for the Fourth, the question is whether we can get together in the spring, and if so where and how and so forth.

Regarding the Fourth: I can't guarantee we'll come, but it already seems kind of like a tradition and it sure is fun. Please assure everyone that I PROMISE NOT TO THROW ANY BIZARRE TANTRUMS OR PICK FIGHTS WITH ADOLESCENTS THIS TIME.* Anyway, I don't really want to commit to coming, because who knows how things will work out and if we can afford it, but it is definitely mentally penciled in.

On a related note, I hope your girls will be making their annual pilgrimage to ND this summer. Actually, it will probably be a lot more fun for them now that we're living in Bismarck, which has a lot more kid activities to offer. Also, we now have a bed surplus, which could be nice for them.

To the point: You and Deborah could come up pretty much anytime. Maybe a Minot excursion could be included. Or you and I could plan something for just us, and do something goofy, like a weekend in Minneapolis or Rapid City. I don't think I can take the whole family to Omaha in the spring if we will also be coming down for the Fourth, but if all the changes make the Fourth look iffy, we could consider a spring trip instead.

What if you brought the girls up for their two week Minot/Bismarck stay in early June, and worked a visit into that?

Also, let's think about a "just men" thing involving hunting this fall.
*The previous Fourth of July, Kevin and I had taken our families to a large field near a ballpark that hosted an annual fireworks display. There was a large crowd. A few people recklessly started setting off

their own fireworks, some of which exploded very near our children. I'm generally a calm and peaceable person, but when my kids were young I could become surprisingly aggressive if I felt they were threatened. On that particular occasion, Kevin actually grabbed me in a bear hug and carried me away from the confrontation, which was a nice thing for him to do, because I was in a full-blown Papa Bear rage. This was quite out of character for me; unless my children are at risk I tend to stay cool even under great stress.

* * *

Date: 4/3/96
From: Reagan
Subject: my own brain dead self

So I've signed on and I'm sitting here feeling pretty disappointed that this whole internet stuff seems like a big load of useless crap except for e-mail. The AOL universe seems to offer nothing that interests me. I'm not quite ready to write off the web yet, but that's mainly because I haven't learned how to browse it well enough to know it well enough to conclude that it's pretty useless too. I think the underlying problem is that AOL and the web are full of humans unburdening themselves of their uninteresting innards.

Is that dark enough?

The real problem is that I always thought it would be cool to sign on every night and write in a journal and send you messages and so forth, but here I am and I'm so tired all I want to do is go to sleep. Brings me back to one of life's great lessons which is that regular sleep habits make everything better and easier.

I'll write again when I'm more awake and less angst-ridden. It's really just bean withdrawal talking anyway.

* * *

Date: 4/4/96
From: Reagan
Subject: jibber jabber blah blah blah

We're going to Minot this weekend. Or else Mom is coming here. It just depends on the weather.

I either want to just sleep for a long time, or else plunge into many fascinating and exciting new activities.

It just depends on the weather.

* * *

Date: 4/5/96
From: Reagan
Subject: Our people on the big screen

Just got back from "Fargo," the new Coen brothers movie. It was disconcerting to see northern midwesterners (or whatever we are up in here in this nonregion) on the screen. The accent and culture were a little overdone, but pretty accurate. The Coens being Minnesotans, North Dakota was portrayed as being a sort of adjunct empty wing of Minnesota proper, but it was nevertheless pleasing and amusing to see "us" in a movie.

One gets so used to seeing other American regional cultures, especially New York and the south, along with LA, to a lesser extent New England, etc., that you sort of come to assume that it is more valid for them to be the subject of movies, or books, songs, and other art. Even the Irish, the English, and other foreign cultures have more a screen presence in American movies than does middle America. I think a German filmmaker made a film that ends up in the northern plains, which I think was called "Stroszek." I saw it in college. It was pretty bleak in that dark European way.

Anyway, "Fargo" is by turns funny and brutal, but I can sort of accept the violence because it really did end up being an important part of what the movie was about. I would certainly recommend it. It made me feel oddly proud, which is perhaps a provincial response. I wonder what people from other parts of the country will make of it.

* * *

Date: 4/6/96
From: Reagan
Subject: Family trips

Did you figure out how to travel happily as a family? Remember how when we were kids it seemed like it was a necessary part of every family trip for everyone to get real tense and for Dad to kind of blow up or get real pissy? I don't think it's that bad for us, but we always end up starting real late and with everyone kind of down and miserable. I wish I could figure out how to break this pattern.

* * *

Date: 4/11/96
From: Kevin
Subject: Finally

Okay, here goes the Great E-mail Response.

I can certainly see why you would feel disoriented, just from your description of that one day. And I know what you mean about alone time. It has been a requirement of mine for a long time, and seems pretty fundamental to my nature. I really hope that you find a way to get more for yourself. It would be good for you and for everyone you interact with. (with whom you interact? Sounds stilted.)

Oh, come on! It just won't be a real Fourth without the threat of physical violence! Where's your pep, boy? But, okay, really, I hope you can make it down, and it seems as though it would make sense to incorporate a pick-up or drop-off of the girls with that trip. I'm thinking at this point that I could do the other end of the girls' visit and spend a few days with you. I like the idea of doing an out-of-town trip, but I'd rather wait until I have more money. Fall hunting thing? Sounds good!

I'm interested in your assessment of the e-universe, as I have not yet done much exploring. For one thing, I'm waiting until I get a faster modem, and for another, I just don't have the urge. It's kind of like with golf: I always feel as though I could be doing something better. I don't think that you should consider your uninterest in the lives of others to be "dark." 99.9% of what goes on in life has been done or said before, and it's that elusive .1% that really makes it interesting. There's no virtue in being satisfied with the same old stuff.

I love your jibber-jabber note. Or I hate it. It just depends on the weather.

I had decided not to see "Fargo," thinking that it would be unnecessarily violent and very likely as misrepresentative of our part of the world as most movies I've seen, but your comments have me reconsidering.

Concerning family travel, I think you've nailed it yourself: a scrambling, late departure is one of the worst enemies. It seems to me that you're all pretty good at the actual travel part, so if you could find a way to a) shop, gas and pack ahead of time (you don't really need to pre-load, but if most everything is packed and sitting near the door, you'll be fine), b) get to bed at a decent hour, c) get up an hour before you think you need to get on the road when you want to, d) eat a quick, simple breakfast, and e) not worry quite so much about how the house looks when you leave, you should do well. I find that planning for departure is as important as planning the trip or vacation itself. I put preparation items on my calendar for the days prior to travel.

Something happened to my mailbox recently, wiping out all the messages that were stored there. Have you sent anything since the Family Trips message? If so, please re-send.

* * *

Date: 4/17/96
From: Kevin
Subject: is easily entertained

So, here I'd given up on The New Yorker, and I found two things worth sharing in the latest issue. This is from an article on Ross Perot:

> Above all, there was the simple and increasingly conspicuous issue of inappropriateness. Nuttism is largely a matter of acting inappropriately. Biting the bishop's wife might be the correct thing to do in one set of circumstances – alone and late at night, aflame with doomed passion, in the conservatory – but the same act committed in, say, a receiving line at St. Paul's Cathedral is crazy. Perot, it became increasingly clear as the 1992 race drew to a close, had a hard time grasping this sort of distinction. He was given to sudden, sharp, disconnected exclamations ("It's just that simple!"; "End of story!"; "Here's the beauty part!") that seemed as if they were meant to be spoken in some other setting, possibly in a parallel universe.

> "He looks attractive until you smell his breath," [a former volunteer] says. "We were all looking for a hero, and he was a hero, but only because we didn't know him better. Everybody is an enemy to him. He is very caustic, very cruel. People were afraid to do anything. The difference between him and crazy is about three billion dollars. I'd be afraid to see him as President of the United States."

The other is a filler item (typos and all):

> [From Avio Forum, the in-flight magazine of Balkan Bulgarian Airlines]
>
> WHY visit The House ot Humour and Satire?
>
> Because your car or bus stops at a free parking. You walk about fitty meters without paying recket. The enter trough the side door (there is no main entrance yet, but it is planned to be built outside the building), confront a funny little ticket office and pay a funny small price for a ticket. Or buy no ticket at all – instead

pay even less and get a book of jokes from Gabrovo, illustrated by Boris Dimovsky. Have you taken a guide? – this will slow you down – choose the language of the tour – Bulgarian, Russian, English, French, German. The guide (mostly a 'She') leads you in the first lobby. The choice is: a strong-nerve and sense of humour test in the Booth of Laughter; the souvenir stand – the only place where you can buy a half cup, a quarter coin, a tea-set for people with moustache, tableware for unwanted guests, useless souvenirs for your love ones as well as specialized issues for humour-albums, catalogues, collections of jokes, short stories and post-cards. The prices have not undergone any changes compared to the outer world and may sound like a joke too. The comes a panorama of crooked, straight and broken mirrors that reflect all you inner faces and thoughts. Then you are kindly asked to the fourth floor – once there you'll understand this strange order of the tour.

* * *

Date: 4/19/96
From: Kevin
Subject: Sinister plots

Tuesday: The third day of the week. [Middle English Tuesdai, from Old English Tiwesdaeg, Tiu's day : Tiwes, genitive of Tiw, Tiu; see Tiu.]

Tiu: The Germanic god of war and the sky.

This sounds MADE UP! I've never heard of Tiu! I don't even vaguely recall a day of the week named after a Germanic god. History is being rewritten! Although, as long as it's being rewritten, I say let's go with the Tuesday Weld idea.

* * *

Date: 4/21/96
From: Reagan
Subject: Just my way of letting you know I'm here

Why are we born, only to grow old and die?

More soon.

*　*　*

Date: 4/25/96
From: Kevin
Subject:

It seems to be so easy to make mistakes when you're looking for the truth – big, glaring errors that you'll kill and die for. This seems to be true especially for religion and politics, less so for philosophy, and less again for science. I'm just writing this down as I think of it, and I wonder now if those areas are the fundamental ones in our search for the truth. What about art, literature, economics? That would make an interesting discussion.

It doesn't seem to matter when or where a religion is created. They all seem to share a need to believe in something insupportable by observable facts, unreasonable by ordinary intellectual standards, unprovable by (and at odds with) scientific methods, and often just plain absurd on the face of it. Is this really necessary? In order to express, and believe in, fundamental truth, is it necessary to enter what appears to be a fantasy world, to live either with one part of your mind at odds with the other, or with the rational, observing mind not working much at all? That seems to be the history of humanity so far.

This appears to hold true for politics as well, with slightly less fantasy and slightly more willingness to slaughter fellow humans. It would be interesting to see a chart showing the reasons for people being killed by other people since the arrival of Homo sapiens. How many for political reasons? How many for religious? In how many cases did the two overlap so much that they can't be separated? Or is there, underneath everything, a simple, primal desire to kill, with many reasons advanced to justify it?

What I wanted to get at is how an individual or a group can come to believe in the absurd with such powerful certainty. It seems so easy for a dream, a revelation, an idea to take root in a person and completely enmesh him in a blinding web of falsehood. Are we to believe that Truth is a variable concept by era, region or individual? If that's the case, it's not much use, is it? Well, I should qualify that. It's certainly useful to the adherents, and especially to the leaders, but it's not much use to me. I don't want the Truth du jour, and I'm afraid that that's what I'll end up with. I'll find myself honking and braying on a street corner, trying to convince passersby that my ass is the true face of God.

I feel like a high-schooler here, passionately ignorant. I feel driven, though, by the same fundamental force that kept me going through the bad years. I can't stop trying to learn and understand, nor do I want to stop. I do sometimes have to pull back and focus on the surface world in order to function on a practical level, but I always feel the tug inside me. As I recall, your list of what's important in life was topped by Truth, and I wish you had more time to devote to it on more than just a personal, practical level.

* * *

Date: 4/26/96
From: Reagan
Subject: Re: is easily entertained

What can I say? The "House of Humor and Satire" bit was just a gem.

Also, I agree with you. The Perot excerpt, especially the part about the bishop's wife, is exactly the kind of writing we've always wanted from the New Yorker. So what's the bottom line: should I subscribe, or not? Do you have any old issues lying around you could mail to me?

An interesting question. How many people have killed or died for philosophy? Or for science? Actually, I suppose quite a number of people have died for science, generally having been killed by people who were killing for religion.

As you know, I don't think religion truly is a fundamental area in the search for truth. In fact, I still view it as a wide detour from that search, or perhaps an alternative to it: a framework of thinking that provides a satisfying substitute for truth. At the moment, I also have a low regard for philosophy. It strikes me as intellectual masturbation. But I am not so sure on this point. It may be philistinism, or sour grapes. I think really good fiction is a better area in which to find truth than religion or philosophy. However, I have long suspected that there is no Truth, only truths, and that Searching for Truth is inherently fruitless. I am not sure on that point, either.

Your comment reminded me of a review I read on a new book. The author asserts that the reason "ordinary Germans" killed Jews during World War II was because they hated them. This has stirred up quite a controversy, and has been generally rejected by historians.

I think that uppercase "Truth" may well be a variable concept, because it may well be just another way of saying "biggest falsehood of all." We may well have to content ourselves with lowercase truths.

Let me try to be less obscure. The search for Truth generally leads people into the realm of religion, philosophy, ideology, etc. I am referring here to Truth as in "the one Truth," the idea that there is a central idea or belief that defines meaning and existence. I have long had grave doubts that such a thing exists. When I say I value truth highly, I am speaking on what many people would consider a "lower" level. Science seeks true answers to questions. I am devoted to the idea of intellectual honesty: that one should seek to discover, believe, and express truth. Not so much the daily honesty of telling someone that yes, their nose really is big and unattractive. In my line of work it is more in the nature of saying "we could try to pretend the statute means that, and we might get away with it, but that's not what it really means, and I won't pretend it does." There is no fundamental "Truth" about what a statute means. Statutes are just chunks of words that are inherently ambiguous. However, they do carry a core range of meaning from which it is dishonest to depart.

What is scary is how people will not just try to twist them in how they use them, but will twist them in their own minds and believe they mean what is convenient or desired. People are so ready, for so little cause, to sacrifice their own recognition of truth, their own honesty in what they think and believe with themselves. That is why faith and ideology so often become repulsive: they are often the ultimate abdication of the individual's commitment and ability to be intellectually honest, to discern and believe what is, rather than what is wished.

Kevin, I am not doing all that well. Perhaps it is because ideas like this are so disturbing to me, that I am just not travelling down the good road. Old patterns, old habituated responses to stimuli, are re-emerging. I am trying to grapple with this.

* * *

Date: 4/26/96
From: Kevin
Subject:

Well, I'm just going to babble on here, and get some of these thoughts down. Obviously, I realize that a world in which only the logical, provable, and physical were present would be a pretty flat world for us humans. I understand the roles that intuition, dreams and imagination play in life. I know what poetic truth is, and have felt the benefits of sublimating consciousness. I know what it feels like to have faith.

Still, I continue to be baffled, not so much by the moral and philosophical teachings of the various religions, but by their seemingly universal insistence on creating versions of history which are indistinguishable from myths, fairy tales and, in some cases, lunatic ravings.

And what's the deal with science? We're all MAGICIANS now, thanks to science, and people just take for granted the fun stuff and ignore whatever conflicts with their belief systems. We can fly; we can look at, talk to, and kill people anywhere on earth; we can create new life forms – CREATE NEW LIFE FORMS! – and people are still going "Yeah, but I still think the world was formed when a giant cat coughed up a hairball."

Of course, science has a mixed record in answering the big questions that religion and philosophy have addressed. It's done a remarkable job in discovering how the earth and the heavens were formed, and how humans were created. It's done a great job in explaining natural phenomena. It's been less effective dealing with why humans do what we do, and what we ought to do, and of very little help in discovering why we're here, what happens (if anything) when we die, and the existence and nature of any higher power or consciousness.

What I'm tottering toward here is the idea of a synthesis of science and religion. I'm not really sure what form that would take, except that it wouldn't be a nature worship/Mother Earth kind of thing. What is needed, I think, is a very special person to start the thing rolling, a scientist/poet/mystic, someone who is honest, insightful, and charismatic.

I know what you're thinking: "The damn fool is quitting writing to become a scientist/poet/mystic!" No, don't fear. I'm not picturing myself in that role.

I've also read about the "ordinary German" controversy. I was surprised to read that the idea upset so many scholars. I have some ideas on the subject, but I don't feel like getting into that right now.

I'm trying to decide how I think of the Truth, and here's what I'm coming up with: rather than one central idea or belief, it is more like a fabric, woven from strands of individual truths.
I'm distressed to hear that you are doing so poorly. A great deal of pessimism seems to have crept into your life. I'll talk to you soon, perhaps even before you read this.

***

Date: 4/26/96
From: Reagan
Subject: is amazed he really needs a subject.

I can't BELIEVE this thing won't let me send a message without a subject line! WHAT A USELESS FEATURE!

Here's the most disturbing thing I have heard in a while. There is a medical term: "de-gloving injury," as in "the patient suffered a de-gloving injury to his left hand." These injuries generally seem to involve farm machinery, oil drilling rigs, or industrial machinery peeling all the skin off a hand. It gives me the big time willies.

Thanks for calling this morning. I really needed that.

By the way, I have a new e-address at work. I don't have it on me. I'll try to remember to send it to you next week.

***

Date: 4/30/96
From: Reagan
Subject: I hate AOL

AOL is toying with me again.* I REALLY DON'T WANT TO GO INTO IT! Please tell me if you receive this and "How ironic, Superman."

*There have been very few times in my life that I have experienced the sensation of hatred, but in 1996 I genuinely hated AOL. The process of accessing AOL via dialup was painfully slow and uncertain; it sometimes took multiple attempts to connect. Then the search process was painfully slow. You had to consider your searched words with care because it took a long time for the results to return. These you would have to consider carefully, because the return list was cryptic, with few clues regarding what was actually on the site, and when you selected one it would take a very long time to load. Long enough to go make a cup of coffee or fold some laundry. If the site

wasn't what you were looking for – which it usually wasn't because there was so little on the internet – you had to repeat the process. Often, just as you found something interesting, AOL would abruptly terminate your connection. Everyone knew they were grossly oversubscribed and that they would kick people off so others could log on. It was infuriating. Yet, every single morning on my relatively short drive to work, there would be ad after ad on the radio inviting even more people to join. And in seemingly every store, and arriving regularly in the mail, were CDs for a free trial membership. When I finally quit AOL, it took six hours on the phone on a Sunday, working through multiple layers of people who were being paid to try to prevent me from leaving. To this day, the memory revives feelings of anger.

9. May 1996: "How ironic, Superman"

Date: 5/2/96
From: Kevin
Subject: I hate AOL

I got "I hate AOL," but not "How ironic, Superman."

I'm leaving this morning (Thursday) for a three-day field trip to Western Nebraska with Emily's class. I'll be back late Saturday night.

I was looking through an old book I have, "Blackstone's Modern Card Tricks and Secrets of Magic." Two things surprised me. One, it covered everything from false shuffles to making an elephant disappear. Two, Blackstone was a pretty big-name magician, and he exposed a lot of popular tricks.

* * *

Date: 5/4/96
From: Kevin
Subject: I'm back!

Had a great time. Tell you about it soon. How goes it there?

* * *

Date: 5/5/96
From: Reagan
Subject: Re: I'm back!

I'm better than bad. I'm glad to hear you're back. Actually, it seems to be relatively noiseless, albeit in a muscular porpoise-like way. What kind of school trip takes one away from home for two days?

May 1996: "How Ironic, Superman"

Too bad you didn't get "How ironic, Superman." It was amusing, I think, in the way one can be amusing only when one is on an emotional cusp. Anyway, it has apparently vanished into the AOL wasteland.

I can't BELIEVE everyone is so excited about the Web. What a great big intellectual vacuum. Just what we needed: a new and more expensive way to waste our lives gabbling brainlessly at each other.

I'm still telling myself I just haven't found all the good parts yet. I hope I will have to eat the above words.

What do you do for fun? How much fun do you have? Why does the word "fun" sound like fun, while the word "fund," which differs almost indiscernibly in pronunciation, sound so stodgy and boring?

Saw the Birdcage. As you say, it was just a pretty funny movie. However, it's playing to packed houses in Bismarck still, and I believe that is a good thing. Familiarity breeds at least some base level of acceptance, that they are humans and have lives.

To bed!

* * *

Date: 5/5/96
From: Reagan
Subject: Please tell me if this works

I am trying to send an attached word processor document. Please let me know if you receive this message and/or the attached short message.

[Two pages of garbled text]

* * *

Date: 5/6/96
From: Reagan
Subject: Nivek Llafup lives!

I played the backwards name game (consisting of saying people's name backwards) with Sabrina the other day, and she loved it. You have the best backwards name by far.

I'm all set now, my man. We've made the master bedroom into a big guest/computer/TV/study room. I got a $50 computer desk at Kmart. It's great! It's about a 20-year-old design, but perhaps because of that it is very sturdy. It uses many sturdy metal fasteners instead of the new small wooden dowel and glue approach. It was a bear to put together, but I am well pleased. Plus, we got a printer about a week ago, a good color jet. So now I have lots of room and a comfortable set up.

We got the printer, and right away Reagan's on it. The first thing he made was a sign in a rather putrid combination of green, red, and purple saying "coller room it mite make you sick." He put it on his bedroom door. Then he made another sign with a big vampire bat on it. We finally pry him off, and Sabrina gets on. What does she make? A sign with flowers all over it saying "SABRINAs room of peace." She liked it so much, she made three more with various lovely borders. Annie asked her if she meant her room was peaceful or if it was a larger message. She was offended, and said it was intended to mean peace for all the world, of course.

Kids! You gotta love 'em!

I may be turning the corner on this thing.

***

Date: 5/7/96
From: Kevin
Subject: Porpoise-man

Actually, the school trip took three days, quite an ambitious undertaking for a fourth-grade class. We visited a number of historical sites that played a part in the Oregon Trail, which stretched from Eastern Nebraska to Western Oregon. (I'm confused. Are Eastern and Western supposed to be capitalized there?) Anyway, I was fairly sure that the whole thing would be underplanned, uncoordinated, of limited educational value, poorly supervised and exhausting.

Happily, I was wrong on all counts. A tremendous amount of time and energy went into planning the trip. So many parents came that the kids ended up in supervised groups of only two or three. The buses were tour coaches, with plush, reclining seats, televisions, and huge windows. The selected tour stops were very interesting and informative, with small museums at most of them. I think that everyone, students, and parents alike, learned a great deal from the experience, some of which just can't come in a classroom setting. I was also nice having some time to get to know the teachers, students, and parents. It was a pleasant social situation.

I feel quite a loss at not receiving "Superman." Would it be worth just a brief hint at the contents, or is it just all gone?

I feel in no rush to Web-surf. Let me know if you find anything interesting.

Do I have fun? Sure I do, although I'd have more fun if I had more funds. I like to run, but I don't like the runs. Etc., etc.

I will try to send back to you what was supposed to be a word processor document. It will have as its subject "This doesn't work." Let me know if you get it.

Yes, I always did enjoy my name backwards. Barb and Tom and I had fun with it in high school ("Brab Krahs" is okay, "Mot Nosredna" is pretty good), and Tom and I still occasionally call each other by our backwards first names.

Really enjoyed the printer story. You have some wonderfully unique children.

* * *

Date: 5/7/96
From: Kevin
Subject: This doesn't work

You may need to Save your word processor documents in ASCII format in order to send them. I was unable to Import your document onto this page, and had to Attach it instead. I'm curious to know what you get. Anyway, when I read your message, the word processor portion started out `/1dQQxAAAAA` ... and went on like that for two pages. Very entertaining.

***

Date: 5/7/96
From: Reagan
Subject: Re: This doesn't work

I will have to see if saving my word processor documents in that format is something I can do. If so I will try it. As far as I can tell, there was nothing attached to your e-mail message. The document was actually only two sentences long, in English.

Re: the backwards names, I remember you, Barb, and Tom doing that, and it has stuck with me for all these years, although whenever I mentally dust it off, no one around me has backwards names as cool as yours and Tom's.

I'm afraid Superman is unreproducible. I started off with me saying how ironic it is that the only thing I could think about at that time was "my troubles" but that I was so sick of thinking and talking about them that I couldn't stand to discuss them in a message. It then segued through a lame attack on Wayne Boring into a bizarre and unexpected passage using the voice of an old woman living an isolated and lonely life, discussing the intended acquisition of an HP DeskJet 660C color inkjet printer with a happenstance visitor.

***

Date: 5/9/96
From: Kevin
Subject: Re: Re

I think I tried Attach before, with a non-ASCII document, and it didn't work then, either. When I tried to send, I got a message that I couldn't send it over the Internet.
Well, I say a sad farewell to "Superman." Start printing your e-mail!

Feeling a little low the past couple of days, for no apparent reason. Just crabby, dissatisfied, unmotivated. Probably just a mood swing.

* * *

Date: 5/9/96
From: Reagan
Subject: Re: is easily entertained

I'm not sure I want to understand the strange order of the tour.

* * *

Date: 5/9/96
From: Kevin
Subject: Huh?

I just got this from you:

I'm not sure I want to understand the strange order of the tour.

* * *

Date: 5/16/96
From: Kevin
Subject: Cruisin'

Doing okay these days, back at work on the self-help book. I did go through a mini-crash, and realized that I had to refocus on writing and get better control of my daily schedule, which had become too unstructured for even my loose standards.

I'll be teaching writing to forty fourth-graders today and Friday, an hour each day. This grew out of conversations with Emily's teacher on the field trip. One of the boys on the bus was quite taken with the idea that I was a writer, and he and I began working on a story, which I hope to help him complete while I'm visiting the school. You know that I've always enjoyed the occasional teaching gig, even back in high school. Did you have Mini Days at MHS? There would be a day or two when hour-long specialty classes would be offered, taught by whoever had an interest in doing so. I can remember doing that, probably on cartooning.

Looks like the ND trip is gelling. As it stands now, we'll travel on Sunday, the 23rd of June. How certain are you, at this point, that you'll be able to come down for the Fourth? I suppose an option would be for the girls to spend the Fourth up there, and for you to come down (or someone from Omaha to come up) to bring the girls back on the weekend.

* * *

Date: 5/16/96
From: Reagan
Subject: A voice echoing back out of the distance

Responding to an old message you sent to me about a message you recently received from me consisting of a single sentence. As I recall, I received an amusing and offbeat message from you, including the article on the House of Humor. It put me in what was, I thought anyway, a fairly frisky and creative mood, and I sent back an ostensibly humorous reply. Anyway, I think it is possible that I sent the one sentence as the first of two or three messages in a single evening replying to the House of Humor message. It seemed creative, but AOL apparently made it even more creative by delaying it in cyberspace for a few weeks. Maybe Superman will show up on your screen eventually after all.

I know just what a "mini crash" is, and what a pain they are. Do you think everyone has them? Will they go away? Will we even out over time? I'm tired of the ups and downs, I truly am, my friend.

Stuff about my work blah blah blah. My life blah blah blah. House car kids, hey aren't they cute! Soccer ballet they sure are special childhood isn't what it used to be where did our lives go.

May 1996: "How Ironic, Superman"

It seems like schools must be a bit more flexible down there. Two-day field trips, guest teachers, that's pretty cool stuff.

I'm not very good at planning for trips. I will run all the dates by Annie, she is good with this stuff. I really like coming down for the Fourth, although the Fourth might be better here in Bismarck in terms of finding good places to set off fireworks, than Fargo was. However, being able to set them off in your own street, now that was great. Will that be possible at either your or Peggy's new houses?

I   just   don't   know   no   no   no

Q: How many dizbusters does it take to screw in a lightbulb?

A: Seven. And they scream the whole damn time.*

The crisis seems to have passed, and my life is either getting better or breaking into even smaller fragments. It's too soon to tell.

*According to Blue Öyster Cult.

* * *

Date: 5/17/96
From: Kevin
Subject: A voice echoing back out of the distance

Yes, them ups and downs. It's beginning to feel like I'm a drug user, except that it's my own body producing the drugs. I was in a Big Downer for a long time, and now I have smaller ups and downs. It's not as though I feel no control over my life or my feelings, but there is that underlying roller-coaster effect that continues to need to be dealt with.

Note from you yadda yadda* usual horseshit blather blather whine and complain . . . no, JUST KIDDING! That was a cruel thing to say. But funny. And that's all that matters.

Yes, Emily's school has been pretty user-friendly. I did the first of my two classes today, and had a lot of fun. It does seem pretty easy to get a bunch of grade-schoolers fired up to use their imaginations, especially in a limited time frame. I did a few basic things on writing, shared The Bomb Speck Hero** with them, and got them going on creating their own comic book stories. Man, the place was really humming for a while, in that quiet, full-bore creative way.

Can't do the fireworks at my place. Not sure about Peggy's, although I'm assuming it's outside the city limits. I could also see us returning to the old neighborhood to set them off.

Loved the BOC joke. A laugh-out-loud treat.

Yeah, the battle still rumbles on. I have the feeling that I have a lot more battling to do, but that's okay. I continue to learn from the struggle.

Interesting, not so much that horseshit is not in Prodigy's speller, but that it suggests horse shit as an alternative.

I have to think that instantaneous message-sending has had an effect on communication, in that there is much less likelihood of a cooling-off period between composition and dispatch. I'm thinking particularly of anger-based messages.***

It was almost a year later, on April 24, 1997, that the Seinfeld episode "The Yada Yada" aired. Precognition?

**The Bomb Speck Hero was a cartoon character I created as a child. He was a fragment of a bomb that came to life from radiation. He was actually the same size as the human characters – sometimes even bigger – so it would have been more accurate to call him The Large Bomb Fragment Hero. He got shot at a lot.*

***More precognition? It's interesting to see how quickly this negative aspect of digital communication became apparent, though I* *don't think anyone foresaw just how vituperative online communication would become. One of the benefits of pre-digital communication methods was that they had inherent buffers for emotional impulses, particularly anger. One might dash off a strongly-worded letter in the heat of the moment, but in the time it took to fold it, put it in an envelope, seal the envelope, put a stamp on it, address it, and take it to be mailed, good judgment might step in and cause a change of heart. It was often advised to put such a letter in a drawer overnight and re-read it before mailing. One might make a phone call while feeling angry, but the ensuing conversation could lead to a mutual understanding or even an apology. In any case, there was much less hate-messaging: the closest we had then was the angry answering machine message.*

* * *

Date: 5/17/96
From: Reagan
Subject: Attachment, the sequel

Please tell me if there is something in English attached to this. I think it is formatted in ASCII, although I got kind of a strange message box that may have been trying to tell me it hadn't worked. I had two ASCIIs to choose from, and I chose the windows rather than the DOS version. Do you "attach" your messages to me, or do you just compose them on line?

Yes, the underlying roller coaster, that's just it. Well, I suppose it's better to have an underlying roller coaster then to be lying under a roller coaster. Hoo haw!

Hey, Bomb Speck! I'd forgotten all about him. That's great!

I was helping Mom do a fund-raising letter for her campaign. I was doing a final spell check. Her name was at the top in big bold letters. I inadvertently directed the spell checker to substitute Peafowl for Pufall. That would have been pretty interesting.

From my experiences in the net, your last comment is absolutely on target. Those angry jerks, they really piss me off. I'd just like to beat the crap out of all of them! Why can't they cool off and get some perspective BEFORE they press "send?" Dickheads!

[Routing information]

This document is formatted in ASCII, whatever the heck that means. Tell me if it is still in English when you receive it. Also, whe&*&&^*&%oiut&= [Three more lines of garbled text]

* * *

Date: 5/19/96
From: Reagan
Subject: More mush from the wimp

The subject line comes from one of my favorite true news stories of all time. In the bleakest days of the Carter administration, the President had delivered yet another dry as dust sermon on some topic. A New York newspaper ran a front-page story on it, and as a joke, a junior guy entered as a headline for the story: "More Mush from the Wimp." Of course, the whole first run went out with that headline. A hullabaloo ensued, though not perhaps quite to the scale that one might have expected. I've always wondered if the guy got into any trouble.

Anyway, for some reason this amuses me enormously. I still laugh about it! I sort of know why, but I can't quite put it into words. The whole incident is just so perfect, and it is a terrific, pithy headline.

There's a help/info button in my AOL e-mail area called "Where's my mail function?" If you say it out loud, it sounds like either an embarrassing confession of anatomical ignorance, or a profound questioning of the role of men in modern society.

* * *

Date: 5/19/96
From: Reagan
Subject: How ironic, Superman

May 1996: "How Ironic, Superman"

I will always associate the word "ironic" with Wayne Boring's Superman. Do you remember that? Actually, his name is pretty ironic.*

What is ironic is that all I can think about is struggling to make my life better, AND I AM COMPLETELY SICK OF TALKING ABOUT IT! So, I want to e-mail you, but the only thing on my mind is a topic I just can't stand to write about anymore.

Why is it such a struggle to live right, and so easy to slide back into living wrong? Some kind of emotional entropic principle? Living right is actually easier than living wrong, but it is somehow harder to stay in that mode. I can't bring myself to try to refine that point.

Yes, I will just let the warm water carry me away, quietly away . . .

I would like to own a Walther PPK .32, just like James Bond's. But then what the heck would I do with it? I wonder if it would be kind of a kick to try to go hunting with something like that. Stalking around the woods in a nice suit and dress shoes.

I bought a computer table Sunday. My, it's nice. Would you care for some pie, young man? Come in out of that hot sun. Why, I hardly ever have anyone to talk to around here anymore. I'm thinking I might just buy myself a printer tomorrow. I believe an HP660C color inkjet would be right nice. Won't the little folk be pleased? Maybe the little buggers will ACTUALLY START USING THIS $2,500 PIECE OF PLASTIC HOUSE FURNITURE FOR A CHANGE!

That was the artist's real name, and in our opinion his name was appropriate to his rather dull, static artistic style. In our youth we haunted garage sales buying used comic books, so we read a lot comics published during the 1960s. The comic book company DC, publisher of famous titles like Batman and Superman, was at a low point, churning out trite, corny stories. They made frequent use of the phrase, "How ironic . . ." usually as commentary delivered toward the end of a story in an attempt to wrap things up with some kind of moral observation. We were big fans of the Marvel comic company, which was in its glory days, launching characters like Spider-Man, The Fantastic Four, Iron Man, The X-Men, and the

Avengers, featuring more interesting extended story lines. We had complete collections of every major Marvel comic, including the coveted first issues, which we later sold for a large sum of money. On a percentage profit basis it is by the far the best investment either of us will ever make.

* * *

Date: 5/19/96
From: Reagan
Subject: How ironic, imbecile

I just found and sent "How ironic, Superman," thus forever robbing it of its cult status as a missing e-mail message. Apparently, when I finished typing it, I clicked "Send Later" rather than "Send." I just did the same thing to another message, and when I tracked it down to the "send later" queue, there was "Superman."

So I don't hate AOL. Uh oh, does this mean I have to hate myself now?

No, I will hate the act, but not the actor.

That didn't sound quite right. Also, there are some actors I hate. Although really, do I truly know them as human? How can one hate what one does not know? Although one cannot truly hate what one truly does know. Hate requires distance and the absence of compassion. It is hard to hate what one understands. That is why when we are filled with hate we passionately resist attempts to help us understand the objects of our hatred. We cherish the power and clarity of our hatred and prefer it to the discomfort of understanding and compassion.

But I digress.

Why don't I learn to dance? It looks like great fun. What do I want to do? Why am I living my life as though it's a narrowing cattle chute with a big hammer at the end?

Cheery enough for ya, matey?

Deer hunting with a Walther PPK. Now THAT would be sporting.*
Martinis after, of course.

Of course I would never actually go deer hunting with a handgun. It would be both illegal and entirely inappropriate.

* * *

Date: 5/23/96
From: Kevin
Subject:

My Dearest Reag-a-deag:

Well, I guess I have some catching up to do. I'm behind in our little game of E-mail tag. (Prodigy's speller doesn't grok "E-mail," "e-mail," "Email," or "email." I have a feeling that it's the weak sister of online services.) Actually, this E-mail business with you is great, a real highlight. I like seeing the little envelope symbol when I log on. It almost always means a message from you, although once in a while there's some feeble ad for an online service.

So, concerning your attaching experiment. Here is the first part of what I received:

This document is formatted in ASCII, whatever the heck that means. Tell me if it is still in English when you receive it. Also, whe&*&&^&%oiut&=

There's more, but you get the picture. Try the other ASCII. When I'm writing short notes to you, I do it online. When it's longer, like this one, I compose it in WordPerfect, store it in ASCII, go into Prodigy, and use the Import feature, which allows me to bring a file into the Write area from outside Prodigy. At that point, it's just like I typed it online.

The teaching thing went very well all 'round: enthusiastic, productive children, pleased teachers (I've been invited back for next year), and a good experience for me, too (working in front of a crowd, ad-libbing, being creative under pressure). One of your features that I've coveted is your talent for being in the spotlight: speaking, performing, whatever. I'd like to get better at it and I think I have it in me to be pretty good.

Dickheads, yes indeed. Well, they built the Internet, and I suppose we should let them enjoy it a little while longer before government regulation and corporate advertising take over. Not a complaint, really, just seeing what's coming.

Hey better to live your life in a narrowing cattle chute with a hammer than shooting cattle for marrow and hamburger. Ha!

Yeah, Wayne Boring. That couldn't have been his real name, could it? It would be fun to find out more about him, but not fun enough to justify even a nanosecond of effort on my part.

I apologize, but I chuckled when I re-read the part where you go: "AND I AM COMPLETELY SICK OF TALKING ABOUT IT!" Sometimes EVERYTHING I'm talking about seems like so much blather, even good, enlightened, open, heart-to-heart stuff. But, what am I going to do, become a monk with a vow of silence? No.

Living right? I know what you mean. The thing is, when you're struggling up from living wrong, there's a point at which you know what it takes to live right; you've figured it out and you can see the future: "If I just do what I know is right, it'll be smooth sailing, or at least a lot better than it was." And, mostly, you'll be right, with big exceptions for the unpredictable behavior of others and the occasional Life Disaster.

But the thing is, what the lay person doesn't realize is how scary precognition is. You see the future, and you're going to be gored by a water buffalo, and there's nothing you can do about it. Scary. But, also, you see yourself moderately happy and relatively well-off, and there's nothing you can do about that, either. You're locked in. A taste of Destiny vs. Free-will. And living sick is more unpredictable, more action-packed; you have to be more nimble. It's an adventure, and you're used to it. Of course, there's more to it than that. There's a dynamic level of health beyond just coping, and there are levels beyond that.

Man, take me with you. We'd have thin, expensive cigars, long coats, fine, leather gloves and matching Walthers. It wouldn't matter what happened after that – it would just be cool.

Yes, "Superman" was worth the wait, especially the last paragraph. Say "Hi" to the little buggers for me.

It's interesting, that "Mush" is as funny as it is because of where it showed up. It would have been nothing in an oppositionist publication.

So, if I get AOL, will I find my mail function? Hell of a feature.

* * *

Date: 5/25/96
From: Kevin
Subject: Miles

I checked, and I have 11,015 miles with Northwest, which, according to the chart, qualifies me for an extra bag of pretzels when I purchase a First Class European ticket. I liked peanuts better, especially the honey-roasted kind. Pretzels are just a step above saltines.

Saltines really seem like the physical definition of "cracker," the basic item at the core of the cracker category. I think that, particularly for many of our generation, saltines and Seven-Up are too closely related to the flu to be consumed by choice.

* * *

Date: 5/25/96
From: Reagan
Subject: Should not be required

This had better work, because the attached message is a big one.

[Nine pages of garbled text]

* * *

Date: 5/25/96
From: Reagan
Subject: Oops . . .

Forgot to save in ASCII before I sent it. Sorry. Here it is again.

[The following message had some garbled characters, and has been cleaned up.]

This is the first line of an attached message. The last line will also be identified. Please let me know if you don't get it all. Well, I'm sure you'll get it. After all, you are both witty and bright. What I meant was, please let me know if you don't receive it all.

Of course, if there are parts you don't get, please also let me know, and I will explain them to you just as though were a moron or something. It's all part of the service, sir. More brandy? May I clean your Walther and gut your deer? Very well. And a fine deer, too, if I may say so. You certainly shot him quite a few times, sir! Of course, a .32 just doesn't have the stopping power of a .300 magnum, but so much more panache, yes indeed, sir, so much more panache!

When I log onto AOL, a cheerful male voice says "Welcome." When I log off, it says "goodbye." There's something about the way "he" says "goodbye" that is a little disturbing, like he's trying to sound cheerful, but he's really a bit disappointed and angry that you're leaving, and maybe you won't be so doggone welcome when you try to come back. Monica hates it. Anyway, I can't decide whether they did that on purpose or not.

What I'm actually leading up to is that when I log on and I have received mail, the voice says, "You've got mail!" He seems very happy about that, but maybe a little more surprised than he should be. Of course I have mail, I'm no pariah! Anyway, as with you seeing the little envelope, it is a day-brightener to hear him say that, although it vexes me a bit that his grammar is so bad. I'd like it a lot better if he said, "you have mail," or if you could select alternate voices, like an English butler saying "You received mail, sir. May I fetch your Walther?"

I could just turn the volume off, I suppose.

Recently, I had my first experience with getting mail that wasn't from you. It was, as you say, a feeble ad. Then truly I was vexed. If the kids and Annie start using e-mail, I will often have false mail-from-Kev alarms. Also, we will lose our privacy. Yikes! Hadn't really thought about that. No wonder I've been in no hurry to teach them how to use this. I wonder if we can set some private channel up. I would think so.

Well, I'm feeling a little guilty here. When I did my ASCII experiment, I typed the first half of the message, and then typed a bunch of gobbledygook symbols on the end as a joke. Of course, I didn't stop to think that the joke wouldn't be at all funny, because you would have absolutely no way to know it wasn't real garble. So, anyway, it appears the attaching experiment was actually a success. This message is typed in PerfectWorks and I am attaching it. If it contains any %(*&(%&^$#*%) ^% at all, please let me know.

I will have to see if I have an import function. The "attach" function is on a big button right there looking at me, so I have been using that.

Man, you must have plucked that "marrow and hamburger" line out off a fourth dimension of creativity! Mighty funny!

Your precognition point was subtle and frighteningly accurate. I really do think that part of my resistance to a happy life is that I am far from satisfied by the prospect. I am just so disappointed with reality that I am unwilling to finally give in and accept it. Even imagining the best course my life could take from here, it still seems like a pointless distraction. But, if you reject reality, you will probably not succeed at living well in reality.

I like the thin gloves and long coats. If it was nippy, we could even wear silk ascots. What about headgear? Fedoras? I think bareheaded is more the Bond look. Squirrels and songbirds beware!

Good point on the "mush." If they had been trying to do it, it wouldn't have amounted to much. Part of what's so funny and perfect about it is so many readers accepted it as a valid and accurate headline in a mainstream paper. All part of the darkness that was the '70s.

My own mail function ain't what it used to be.

So that's why I never crave 7-Up.

In the previous line, the word "that" is underlined. Let me know if the underline comes through.

Remember childhood food fads? I think you did green olives for a while. Once, I saw a cartoon strip in which Beetle Bailey was eating saltines, and it hit me just right. For many months, maybe even years, after that, I regularly ate copious amounts of saltines as a snack. If you get about a half dozen in your mouth, you can chew them into a pulp that has a very satisfying texture and consistency. The secret to enjoying saltines is to place them whole on your tongue with the salty side down.

So many things now seem unworthy of even a nanosecond of my effort. I seem to have lost all interest in watching television, and I'm even sort of forgetting why I used to want to go to movies so much. Lately, when I've seen a movie, I walk out of the theater feeling like "well, there went another ten dollars of my money and another two hours of my life." Mowing my lawn, decorating my house. I'm like a cheesy actor asking the director: "What's my motivation here?"

I'm trying to simplify, simplify my non-work life. More reflective time needed. Well, I'm not actually trying to simplify my life, I'm thinking about trying to simplify my life.

Model rockets: the gift that keeps on giving. I took the rocket you gave me to my den meeting a few weeks ago, and as I think I told you, we did manage to get the thing done just barely by the end of the meeting, and it flew great, but it sort of disintegrated/exploded at apogee. I think it was because the glue wasn't dry. So I bought another rocket, and put it together with epoxy. I took it to a den meeting, but I was mixed up, there actually wasn't a den meeting that night, so it was just me, Reagan, and one other scout. I had two engines left from the original starter kit (your gift to me!) so they each launched it once, and it was perfect. No wind, it flew great, floated gently to the earth on its parachute.

Then last Monday was the last den meeting of the year. I had bought three more engines, twice as powerful as the originals (of course), and I really wanted the boys to be able to use them. It was pretty windy, so we went to a really big field, essentially four soccer fields side by side. We went to the windward corner and did an angle launch into the wind. It flew amazingly fast and high, just vanished into the sky. When the parachute popped, you could barely see it. Everything looked fine, although it did drift right off the field, across the street, and into some houses.

Reagan found it in a backyard. It had been blown apart! The tube was shot, blown right in half, and the fins were cracked and distorted. I think I had packed the parachute too tight. I believe there is a charge at the top of the engine tube that blows back up into the rocket tube, blowing the parachute out the top. It had pretty well blown the rocket apart. The boys really wanted to use those other two engines, and I had the epoxy with me, so I figured, what the heck. I glued it back together as well as I could, using ample glue.

The boys got itchy. They were all downwind at the far end of the field except for the two who hadn't gotten to launch it yet. The glue was only half dry, but time was running out, so I slipped it on the launch pole. There was a mom and dad watching with a little girl. I warned them I wasn't really sure what to expect and to be prepared to hit the deck, but they didn't seem to take me too seriously and looked relaxed. I had strong premonitions of disaster. Those engines are powerful! But, I couldn't stop myself, I let the boys launch it. It flew pretty well, in a sort of wild hissing spiral, but upwards. The spiral took some pace off it, so it didn't go so high, which was great, as it didn't drift off the field. The fact that the parachute was half fouled helped too. What amazed me was that it didn't come apart. So we flew it again, with similarly successful results. The boys were delighted, and their first year of cub scouts ended on a perfect note.

So, good gift! Thanks! I have the launcher from the starter kit, which is the main expense. I'm going to experiment with different rockets and engines.

Steven Wright-isms:

How can there be self-help "groups"?

If white wine goes with fish, do grapes go with sushi?

Is there another word for "synonym"?

Just before you get nervous, do you have cocoons in your stomach?

When sign makers go on strike, is there anything written on their signs?

When your pet bird sees you reading the newspaper, does he wonder why you're sitting there staring at the carpeting?

Where do forest rangers go to get away from it all?

Why isn't there mouse-flavored cat food?

Why do they report power outages on TV?

Why are builders afraid to have a 13th floor but book publishers aren't afraid to have a Chapter 11?

That is the end of the Wrightisms. This is the last line of the attached message.

* * *

Date: 5/26/96
From: Kevin
Subject: Oops . . . indeed

Well, I suppose I should have actually looked at your first message before printing it – I got nine unreadable pages. It's a little hard to tell where the intentional stuff is. Ha ha.

The second one was mostly readable, the only exception being punctuation and carriage returns. Apostrophes came out as =92, soft (end of line) returns as =, hard (end of paragraph) returns as =0D, open quotes as =93, and close quotes as =94. There are three ASCII options in my version of WordPerfect. The one I use is ASCII (DOS) text (*.*). You must have access to online help – why don't you MAKE USE OF IT! Oops . . . was I shouting?

Please remember: I'm not just witty and bright; I'm pretty and witty and bright.

Alright, there ARE parts I don't get, like "`/1dQQxAAAAA1Cg`." Where do you get off with that shit, you loathsome toad! The last time anyone said "`/1dQQxAAAAA1Cg`" to me (and meant it), I took him deer hunting and filled him full of slugs! Get my drift? "Moron"?! I oughtta . . . oh, brandy? Why, thank you . . . thank you so much. Yes, here's my Walther . . . you're too kind. Sorry I was so . . . oh, "panache" . . . really, you're much too kind . . .

I'm all over the place with this "hello" and "goodbye" stuff, and none of it seems worth saying.

With Prodigy, every family member can have a different ID and password, so the mail can be kept separate. AOL must offer a similar feature.

"that" was not underlined. Underlining and italics disappear when I import a file, so that's why I use uppercase for emphasis.

Now that you mention it, I can remember you doing the saltine wad thing. You'd end up with a big, doughy lump you'd kind of let dissolve in your mouth.

I've been feeling the same way about the entertainment media, especially videos. Whenever there arises a time period that seems appropriate for entertainment, I think of a trip to the video store, but these days thoughts similar to yours immediately follow – it's time and money wasted. I guess I'm lucky, in that I'm not suffering from motivation deficit at the moment. The writing, and a sense of heading in and exciting direction in general, are keeping me going.

Swell rocket story. Making a bunch of kids happy is a great feeling, especially when it's something they don't ordinarily get to do.

Also enjoyed the Wright stuff. Where did you get it?

* * *

Date: 5/26/96
From: Reagan
Subject: Here we go again

I guess I kind of blew off your earlier suggestion that I try ASCII DOS because we are both, as far as I know, in Windows, but it sounds as though you may have been right. Attached is a short text in ASCII DOS. Let me know how it looks.

Did you know that computer illuminati pronounce ASCII "asky"?

The Wright-isms came from a person at work who periodically distributes "bulk humor" e-mails she receives from some outside source.

[Attached message still had some codes showing.]

The Sufis say that truth can only be spoken with love, and that every word we speak must first pass through three gates: At the first gate we must ask ourselves, "Are these words true?" If so, we let them pass on. At the second gate we ask, "Are they necessary?" At the last gate we ask, "Are they kind?"

10. June 1996: A Marvelous Time

Date: 6/1/96
From: Kevin
Subject:

Some improvement in the attached text. The only codes showing now are for quotes and soft returns.

Really excited about your book suggestion. Seems like it would really add dimension to the thing. I wish you had more time to work on the idea yourself, since we've always wanted to collaborate on a project. In any event, when I get back to work on the book, I'll certainly experiment with the idea.

* * *

Date: 6/2/96
From: Reagan
Subject: Re: No Subject

I'm a little vexed that the attaching thing is still not 100% successful. I will experiment further.

I wish I could say that I would work on that book augmenting idea, but I have at least come far enough in my life to avoid making commitments I am not sure I can keep. If I can, I will.

Had kind of an interesting experience today. Sabrina's dance school was supposed to perform on a big elevated area on the front steps of the Capitol building at 3:00 today. I was musing about what audience there would be. Turned out to be a fund-raising event for the American Cancer Society. People were raising money by seeing how many times they could run around that huge loop in front of the Capitol in one hour. Various performers had volunteered to entertain them, which is where the dancers came in. So it was kind of a weird scene, with various volunteers running different aspects of the event, and people running and walking around the loop, and parents and passers-by milling around, and then there are these dancers dancing on the steps in bright sunlight. It was very enjoyable, with just the right edge of quirky oddness to the whole scenario.

Some of the older dancers did a retro kind of late '60s early '70s dance to "Aquarius" in tie-dyed bell bottom type outfits. It was very well done, actually enjoyable and cool in a direct way, not in an "isn't that impressive for local teenagers" way. As it was going on, it started to rain, harder than a sprinkle, but not so hard to be unpleasant. It was still bright warm sunshine: a "sunshower." It fit the dance perfectly, and ended as the dance did. So it had a happy magical quality.

Two dances later, some littler kids get up to do their dance, and they took their starting positions sitting on a long park bench wearing brightly colored raincoats with hoods. Out of nowhere, as if on cue, this incredible rain and hail storm blasted in, and, as of one mind, everyone in sight stopped whatever they were doing and dashed for this sheltered area where a street runs under the big front steps, volunteers in t-shirts, parents and passers-by, in this tunnel with rain and hail coming down outside in a solid wall.

(Everyone except Reagan D. Instead of running for the tunnel, he ran for a natural "fort" he had found earlier in a nearby grove of trees. Even that proved insufficient for his taste, and he ventured out into the hail and rain, and apparently caught a pretty big hailstone right on the top of his head, because he was complaining about it when we found him wandering around, soaked but happy, when we came out of the tunnel.)

The storm blew over in about five minutes, and in about another five minutes it was bright warm sunshine again. The kids made some buttons and origami, and we all went home well satisfied.

A marvelous time, in an offbeat disorienting way.

* * *

Date: 6/2/96
From: Reagan
Subject: A new approach

Tell me how this looks. Any codes showing? (How gauche!) I'm "trying" everything I can think of, in terms of returns, CAPITALIZATION, punctuation, etc. If this works well, there will be no more ASCII nightmares in my future.

* * *

Date: 6/2/96
From: Kevin
Subject: Re: a new approach

HEY! (It) "worked," alrighty?!

Don't fret about the book. I'm much happier knowing that you're being cautious with your commitments. I began using that tool some years back, and it has been a great help in keeping my life manageable.

Really enjoyed your description of the events on Saturday. I'm always happy to read these glimpses of your life.

Talked to Mom, sounds like travel plans are getting solid.

* * *

Date: 6/5/96
From: Reagan
Subject: Dear Gh'exiwn

That is how your name is spelled according to a new system of phonetics I just made up as I went along, which I think must be the same approach they used in coming up with the new westernized spellings for Chinese place names. Basic message: "Here's an unfamiliar and confusing new spelling that doesn't sound any more like the actual pronunciation than the old spelling did."

The editors of Black's Law Dictionary have taken an even more creative approach: they explain the pronunciation of Latin legal phrases by providing a translation in Greek. Actually, it only looks like Greek. It's really the world's worst phonetic system, invented by medieval monks as part of an effort to maintain their monopoly on the Latin language by preventing ordinary people form ever being able to learn how to pronounce it.

For example, you might think that having "nisi" translated as "naysay" helps, as, surprisingly, it apparently rhymes with "they say." But no! According to the pronunciation guide, "naysay" rhymes with "high sigh!" That's right, it's "ay" as in "aye aye, cap'n!"

This is right in line with "aw" meaning "ow," "iy" meaning "ee," "ir" meaning "eer," and so forth. Why are linguists so stupid?

Black's is so pathetic. When you see a lawyer quoting Black's, which is rare, you know he's scraping the bottom of the barrel big time.

Well, hasn't this message turned into a little festival of positive feelings?

I refuse to send you a birthday card until I at least have the decency to send you your gift. So comb the contents of this envelope for a card in vain! If nothing else, you can build up a nice static charge and then hang shavings from them. It's a magico-scientific stunt you can enjoy right in your own home!

***

Date: 6/6/96
From: Kevin
Subject: Gh'exiwn (the artist formerly known as Kev)

Yeah, what the hell went on with Chinese place names? I've wondered that myself. Was it really worth the effort and confusion? Or was it just slipped through somehow by some bored, anal drone? And speaking of drones, I have to agree that the phonetics guide was worse than useless. The rule should be that you could put a sheet of phonetically spelled text on a lectern and have someone of average education and moderately high speaking ability step up and read it cold. My guess is that this stuff is of use and interest to other linguists only.

My birthday! Ha! I scoff on your lapel! Ha!*

Well, gotta go. I'll get to your memo and the very helpful book comments soon.

*The only thing I remember about Rowan and Martin's Laugh-In that still strikes me as funny is Dick Martin saying to Dan Rowan, "I scoff on your lapel!" and then leaning over and saying, "Ha!" on Dan's lapel. I wish I could use that more often.

11. July 1996: Maybe in My Next Life

[There is a weeks-long gap between the preceding and following messages, due to my visit to North Dakota with Deborah and the girls, followed by the visit of Reagan's family to Omaha for the Fourth.]

Date:7/11/96
From: Kevin
Subject: Reagville. Population: you.

Great conversation. Seems like it's a mighty long haul, to get where we're going. Glad you're with me.

I'll mail Monica's glasses and WordPerfect tomorrow. Did you bring the video camera with you, and do you remember where you left it?

Sarah and I have gotten back to Myst. Thanks for the helpful notes. The main problem seems to be skipping off to other worlds and getting stuck there.

I have a joke for you, but it'll work better on the phone. Ask me.

* * *

Date: 7/13/96
From: Kevin
Subject: U

Found the camcorder. Thanks for bringing it.

My modem isn't fast enough to surf, so I thought you might like to try these Web sites and let me know if they're any good:

http://www2.islandnet.com/-cwalker/
http://spinn.thoughtport.com/spinnwebe
http://www.theonion.com.www.html

* * *

Date: 7/17/96
From: Kevin
Subject: . . . TIMING!

It finally felt like the right time to read "The Inner Game of Tennis" a few days ago. I've been showing Deborah how to play, and I thought I could get a lot out of the book by putting its lessons into practice right away. I only got a few pages into it, though, up to "Letting Go of Judgments" (which sounds a lot like a point in my book). However, what I read struck me more as sleight-of-hand with words than useful information.

He describes a scene in which Mr. A is serving to Mr. B, and Mr. C is umpiring. Mr. A's serve goes out, and is called so by Mr. C. Gallwey describes the action thus:

> Seeing his serve land out . . . Mr. A frowns . . . and calls the serve 'terrible.' . . . Mr. B judges it as "good" and smiles. The umpire neither frowns nor smiles; he simply calls the ball as he sees it.
>
> What is important to see here is that neither the "goodness" nor "badness" ascribed to the event by the players is an attribute of the shot itself.

One part of this is the sense in which the words "good" and "bad" are used. It is certainly common in sports to use them as purely physical descriptions. In this case, all three participants correctly view Mr. A's serve as "bad," since it went out of bounds. "Badness" is an attribute of the shot itself.

In another sense, the words could be used to describe how the shot affected each of the participants in their roles in the game. Now, the shot is "bad" for Mr. A, "good" for Mr. B, and neutral for Mr. C. And again, in my opinion, these are correct views.

In yet another sense, the words could describe how the shot reflected on Mr. A. He may think "I served badly," while the other two think "he served badly." If he continues to miss his serves, he could end up thinking "I'm a bad server." Even here, though, the meaning of that sentence could vary widely, depending on the moral weight that Mr. A attaches to the word "bad." If he uses it in a strictly mechanical way, meaning "I regularly hit the ball out-of-bounds" he is simply being an honest observer of his actions. If he means "I am a failure in this facet of tennis, and it reflects poorly on me as a person," he gets to the point that I think Gallwey is trying to make, that such judgements are counterproductive, in tennis and in life in general.

Anyway, his handling of this example irritated me and stopped me cold. Do you think it would be worth it for me to read on?

* * *

Date: 7/19/96
From: Kevin
Subject: TIMING! And REPETITION!

I was looking through a B. Kliban book that I hadn't seen before, and one of the cartoons, concerning an interview of Ghandi by a Western journalist, contained a note to the effect that the dialogue was not fictitious. This is it, as accurately as I can remember:

Journalist: "What do you think of Western civilization?"

Ghandi: "I think it's a good idea."

* * *

Date: 7/22/96
From: Kevin
Subject:

Mom copied some pages from The Book of Lists that concerned writing and left them for me. Under "The Original Titles of 27 Famous Books," we find that the original title for "The Time Machine" was "The Chronic Argonauts." Also, oddly enough, the original title of "Catch-22" was "Catch-18."

Another amusing item, this one from The New Yorker:

> THAT'S TOO BAD DEPARTMENT
> [From the Times]
> Narcolepsy may be more prevalent in women than thought.

* * *

Date: 7/23/96
From: Kevin
Subject: Hey!

Hey! Sad Boy! Talk to me! Just send along a vulgar, two-word message so I know you're still there.

Had a great conversation with Annie the other day. That gal's got insight aplenty, and touched on a number of things about my life that I've been thinking myself lately. I sure appreciate her concern.

* * *

Date: 7/24/96
From: Reagan
Subject: Re: No Subject

Ha ha ha ha ha ha.

Sorry I've been such an unresponsive schmoe. I'll try to become a more responsive schmoe.

* * *

Date: 7/24/96
From: Reagan
Subject: Re: Hey!

OK, maybe I'm back now.

Sometimes every little thing in life, like turning on the computer and logging onto AOL, just seems so unbearably hard, I can't even contemplate doing it at all. I'd like to just sit still for a REALLY long time.

In answer to your many messages:

Thanks for the glasses and the WordPerfect. I thought I would back-up all my software before loading it on, in case it carried some filthy virus, and, as you know, that was a fiasco. So I'm going to just go ahead and load it this weekend.

My life is a FRENZY.

Yet, it's boring.

I want Myst, but fear owning it.

If I could even imagine myself going to the post office, I would mail a hard copy to you. Maybe in my next life.

It probably wouldn't be worth it for you to keep reading the book. As I well know, when the writing rankles one in that way, it's hard to get anything out of it. It's too bad though, as the book has had a significant positive impact on my life, and in fact the very example you cite has turned out to be a key insight for me in all aspects of my life, although I all too often lose sight of it.

The Ghandi quote was great.

If I had any creative or clever thought in my head, I would share it with you. Maybe next time.

Thanks for your tenacious messaging.

* * *

Date: 7/26/96
From: Kevin
Subject:

Sorry to hear about FRENZY, etc. Wish there was more I could do.

Re: sending me a copy of my message. With Prodigy, I can just e-mail your messages back to you if I haven't deleted them yet. It's definitely not worth a trip to the Post Office.

I'm amazed at how far you got with Myst in such a short time. You really do have a capacity to crank it out.

* * *

Date: 7/27/96
From: Kevin
Subject:

A few things I've been meaning to tell you.

I keep watching myself, when Reag and Sabrina are around, to avoid typecasting them as hypermasculine and hyperfeminine, but they continue to provide plenty of evidence. When we were out lighting fireworks with our cigars, Sabrina not only expressed personal disgust with the idea, she also continually hounded you with her concern for your well-being. Reag had no such problems, and actually seemed to be relishing the idea, walking around with a stogie like a little Huck Finn.

The girls found me reading an article in a low-end women's magazine, and told me that I was "just like Uncle Reag. He'll read anything."

Thanks also to you and Annie for your comments on my book outline. I'm looking forward to going through them one-by-one and incorporating them. Looks like a lot of good stuff. I especially like your comment on television: "Satan!" And I really appreciate Annie's long note on the role of family in creating or curing depression.

* * *

Date: 7/27/96
From: Reagan
Subject: Re: No Subject

Q: How many Gilligans does it take to screw in a lightbulb?

A: They don't have any lightbulbs on the island. IT WAS A TRICK QUESTION!

* * *

Date: 7/27/96
From: Reagan
Subject: Re: No Subject

In response:

1. Reagan actually smoked quite a bit of that cigar. I had to go keep yanking it out of his mouth. And Sabrina was very worried about me. Anyone who thinks gender traits aren't at least 50% genetic has never had children. I try not to reinforce gender stereotype behavior in the twins, but to some extent I end up doing so just by relating to them as they are. We are preaching feminine equality quite hard to Reagan, but I don't know if he's buying it. He'd better. The girls in the under-sixteen set right now are not prepared to accept even the slightest prejudice.

2. Mea culpa: It's true that I will read anything. Monica buys People magazine now, and I mock it, but then I read the darn thing in the bathroom. My secret shame.

3. If television is Satan (which it is), then the televised Olympics are some unknown demon of even greater evil. Everyone at work is walking around like a zombie because no one's getting to bed on time.

I will try to initiate a message, as opposed to simply replying, soon. Right at this moment, it just seems like way too much effort. Sorry. I will try to send back your missing message, which is in my trash list right now.

* * *

Date: 7/28/96
From: Kevin
Subject: Thanx, and a tip of the cyberbeanie . . .

There must have been at least one episode in which the Professor, using coconut fibers and the vacuum in Gilligan's head, created a crude lightbulb so that Ginger could apply her makeup for the Christmas gala. Look for it on video.

I am now going through your book comments and incorporating them. Next to "Fear," you wrote "Ask me for the 'Defending Your Life' quote." Okay, I'm asking.

Also, both you and Mom have advised caution in how I word the autobiographical portion, and I can see the merit in that. If you were me, writing this book, how would you respond to, "Tell me about your experience with depression. How did you come to be depressed?"*

The short answer is that I had an inherited tendency toward depression, compounded by a very difficult relationship with my father.

* * *

Date: 7/30/96
From: Reagan
Subject: Re: Thanx, and a tip of the cyberbeanie . . .

Of course, the smell of burning coconut fibers attracted headhunters from the next island, and then what hi-jinks ensued!

July 1996: Maybe in My Next Life

If you have not seen "Defending Your Life," rent it promptly. If the mood is right, and it hits you right, you'll love it. If not, it will seem promising but clunky.

Anyway, the central idea of the movie is that our challenge on earth, before we die and are reincarnated, is to overcome fear. As much as I enjoyed the movie when I first saw it, I thought that concept was badly flawed. Overcoming fear just did not seem like the central thing. However, in the years since then, it seems more and more on the mark; that an unhealthy response to fear is behind many behaviors that would not immediately seem linked to fear.

Anyway, here's the quote that I transcribed from the movie, and that I find inspiring:

> Fear is like a giant fog. It sits on your brain and blocks everything: real feelings, true happiness, real joy. They can't get through that fog. But you lift it, and buddy, you're in for the ride of your life.

Actually, that speaks so directly to what I'm experiencing right now, that I'm going to have to reflect on that again now.

In response to your question: if I were you writing the book, and I asked me to respond to that question, I'd probably say: "Why am I talking to myself? Maybe my problem isn't depression but rather a multiple personality condition." OOOOOh Ha ha ha ha! I'm so funny! I KILL me! Hey, watch it, that's even worse than talking to yourself!

The thing is, I'm not sure I was ever all that depressed. I mean, there have been times when I've been immobilized, but it's been more of a sort of numb zombie state than a depression. More of a withdrawal or shutting off. I know that same behavior can be caused by depression, but for me I don't think I was immobilized by depression, but just by checking out, by shutting down. I was worried, frightened, anxious, sad, angry, frustrated, etc., but rarely really depressed. Well, I have to go, ask me again next time, maybe I can answer more helpfully.

***

Date: 7/31/96
From: Kevin
Subject: What did Bob Denver do before Gilligan?

Yes, I have seen and enjoyed "Defending Your Life" a number of times. It isn't as good as it could have been, but it still works. I also benefit from becoming conscious of my fears and working to eliminate them.

Anyway, what I was getting at with my questions was "What should I (Kevin) say about my emotional history as it relates to writing the book? What should I tell publishers and, at some point, readers and interviewers, about my past?"

12. August 1996: What Not to do When You're Depressed

Date: 8/3/96
From: Reagan
Subject: He was Maynard on Dobie Gillis

That's a pretty tough question. Your authority for writing the book rests on your own experiences with depression, so you will have to refer to them, and what you learned in the process. Can you draw a line between talking about your experiences with depression as opposed to the causes of the depression? I could see two benefits to not talking about the causes. First, readers who are depressed for some other reason may tend to discount your advice based on their depression being different from yours. It might give them a reason to reject your advice, to see it as not being relevant to them. This is probably not valid, but it could weaken the helpfulness of the book. It would make it less universal. In other words, some aspects of dealing with depression may be pretty universal, but the causes of depression, I would think, may be quite varied.

Second, the more autobiographical the book is, the more it might look to a publisher as being more in the nature of being a personal unburdening, as being a part of your own personal "therapy" that you are working through, rather than as being an actual publishable book. I didn't express that very clearly. I am thinking of a screening reader for unsolicited manuscripts getting a little into it and then saying "well, this guy has some stuff of his own to work through, but I'm not going to read it. He can tell it to his shrink."

Third (yes, this is the third of the two reasons I referenced earlier), there is always the chance you would come to regret having made revelations in print. Of course, just writing the book brings some risk of that with it, and you can't be too inhibited by that, but I can see that talking about your experiences and what you learned from it may be in a different category than particular autobiographical details about our family.

Does that help any? I haven't really put a lot of thought into this. I got strep yesterday and slept about 20 hours so my brain is kind of fuzzy right now.

I really have to pull myself together. Where are those darn bootstraps?

* * *

Date: 8/4/96
From: Kevin
Subject: Ah. I'd forgotten.

Thanks for the fuzz-filtered opinions. I had been considering the first and third of your two ideas, but I hadn't come up with the second. As always, your comments are well-reasoned and helpful. As I've worked on the book recently, I've been experimenting with giving less information on the causes of my depression while using more positive anecdotes to illustrate specific points throughout. So far, this feels pretty good. I wanted the book to be as universal as possible from the start, and I think you're right, that too much detail about the causes could weaken that universality.

You were also right about the new version of "Sabrina." We rented it last night, and it was just wonderful. This is a bit of a backhanded compliment, but I expended the least amount of effort in a long time in getting involved. As you said, the current level of movie-making craft was in evidence, including the many nicely done supporting roles. I'll have to get the original sometime to compare.

We also saw "Independence Day" recently, and it was exactly what I'd heard it would be and expected it to be: a hugely flawed but diverting entertainment. There were a couple of spots that felt like the times when you're on a plane and hit a downdraft and the plane suddenly lurches. It was almost like a subliminal message had just flashed on the screen: THIS IS ENTIRELY WRONG. THIS IS NOT AT ALL WHAT WOULD REALLY BE HAPPENING. That kind of movie-watching takes a bit of effort.

From The New Yorker:

> CORRECTION OF THE WEEK
> [From the Newton (Mass.) News Tribune]
> In the City Beat section of Friday's paper, firefighter Dwight Anderson was misidentified. His nickname in the department is "Dewey." Another firefighter is nicknamed "Weirdo." We apologize for the mistake.

Also in The New Yorker, an interesting article on Bob Dole's campaign, titled "The Minimally Acceptable Man." The caption under a drawing of him: "Bob Dole's refusal to properly pretend runs so deep that it cannot be hidden." From the article:

> Watching Bob Dole campaign for the Presidency is a curious and dislocating experience, like showering clothed or eating naked. It isn't unpleasant, but you can't escape the sense that the thing is at odds with itself." [Although I've done both, and enjoyed myself.] Campaigning on a national scale is largely about pretending – pretending that you are really interested in the stump speech you must give three or four or five times a day . . . Great political performers, such as Bill Clinton, are great because, on some level, they aren't pretending . . . Dole hates it so much that he can hardly bring himself to go through the motions, and even then he cannot resist uttering subversive remarks, in a kind of sidelong running commentary, that make it clear that he's aware of the sham of what he is doing.

> Recently, the candidate's brain trust came up with a campaign slogan designed to highlight its core idea that Dole is a good

enough man to serve as the nation's leader, and that Clinton is not. The slogan is "Bob Dole: A Better Man for a Better America." It is a decent enough slogan, and a normal candidate would have woven it into the flow of his daily verbiage in a dozen different way. In several days of listening to Dole speak in the Midwest, I heard him mention it only once, and that was in an interview, and this is how he described it: "'A Better Plan, A Man for a Better America' – whatever that slogan is they're working on." What you have in Bob Dole is a politician whose refusal to pretend that he gives a damn about the business of marketing himself is so profound that he can't bring himself to memorize his own bumper sticker.

Dole is the nega-candidate . . . He's never going to be able to sustain any sort of movie version of himself, never going to be able to remember to pretend for more than a few minutes at a time. If his handlers insist on stripping his subversive qualities from his public performance, there won't be anything there at all . . . if Dole has a chance – and he does – his self-subversion is the only reason. After four years of the President as a bond salesman, there is something sneakily, cumulatively refreshing about a man who can't be bothered to keep up the pretense that he really cares whether you like him . . . But it's a perverse way to get to be President.

* * *

Date: 8/4/96
From: Reagan
Subject: Second thoughts about Dole

That passage from The New Yorker about Dole as a sort of anti-candidate made me think of him favorably for the first time in about ten years. I would love to hear a candidate make a speech, saying something like: "You know, blah blah blah. You've heard it all before. Just hear what you want to hear. I'm better, for whatever reason you have in mind. Vote for me, vote for me, vote for me. I'm really not going to waste your time, or my time, blabbing about whatever.

August 1996: What Not to do When You're Depressed

I'll do the job, and I won't lay a bunch of crap on you all the time. Face it, you'll have no way of knowing whether I'm doing a good job anyway."

Dole isn't quite up to this level, but he's getting into the neighborhood. He isn't honest in some clean and refreshing way. It's not that he rejects pretense and hypocrisy, it's more like he knows that it's ALL pretense and hypocrisy, and just doesn't really give a rip anymore. He could just as well say one thing as another, and he knows it all too well. What do you say when you know that anything you could possibly say is all crap?

That's a big piece of why I bailed out of politics.

I be golfing. It's fun. It's a really good meaningless diversion from the realities of life. Whack! Man, when that ball takes off like that, it feels mighty good. Whackity whack!

What not to do when you're feeling depressed: spend an entire afternoon in bed thinking about what you'd do if you won one hundred million dollars.

Another one: staring in the mirror at all your facial features until you're just pretty well wigged out from staring at yourself, and feel completely alienated and directionless, like you can scarcely comprehend the fact of your own existence as an individual.

I think collecting things is inherently bad.

The women's Olympic basketball games rocked! The men's sucked! Sports in which it is actually more enjoyable to watch women than men: basketball, diving, golf, tennis, volleyball. There may be many more. Diving is obvious. Women's basketball is a lot more like basketball was supposed to be. Women's tennis and volleyball have longer, more interesting points. Professional female golfers are playing a game that looks like a superbly played version of the game that amateur men play rather than a different game entirely as men's professional golf does. If people would just get tuned into it, women's sports could really take off. Plus, most male athletes are rich jerks. The worst kind!

* * *

Date: 8/6/96
From: Kevin
Subject: That guy in the mirror . . .

If you had one hundred million dollars, would you run a campaign like the one you described? That would be great, and you are one of very few people who could sustain it, under the right circumstances.

There's a book idea: What Not to Do When You're Depressed.

1. Eat anything ending in "os" (Fritos, Cheetos, Doritos, Ho Hos . . .)

2. Watch anything ending in "vision"

3. Come within ten feet of a couch

I saw very little of the Olympics (a little swimming, the Women's Gymnastics whoop-de-do, the bombing), but I found your comments intriguing. Maybe these Olympics were a step up in visibility and viability for women's sports in general.

I used Sarah's computer to try to visit the Web sites I listed for you earlier. The only one I was able to get through to was Spinnwebe, which was boring-to-mildly amusing. The best parts were the ones in which the guy running it goes on about how much he dislikes the incorrect use of apostrophes and quotes, and gives examples of same.

* * *

Date: 8/7/96
From: Kevin
Subject: is jammin' the groove, baby!

August 1996: What Not to do When You're Depressed

I got the "Stop Making Sense" CD last night, and I'm listening to "Burning Down the House" on headphones right now (5:45 am). Aural coffee!

From the Far Side calendar:

> After being frozen in ice for 10,000 years, Thag promotes his autobiography. (Book title: "It was Very Cold and I Couldn't Move").

We'll have to get fax machines at some point. Or, even better, scanners. There's a lot more we can do with this.

The Prodigy spell-checker doesn't recognize "fax." Duh.

* * *

Date: 8/7/96
From: Kevin
Subject: apparently has nothing better to do.

I'm looking through the "Stop Making Sense" booklet:

> Violence on television only affects children whose parents act like television personalities. Civilized people walk funny. Nuclear weapons can wipe out life on Earth, if used properly. Body odor is the window to the soul. The best way to get rid of unwanted flying insects is to have strong body odor. There is always something on television. U.S. money is the worst looking money in the world. People would rather watch things than eat.

What is this crapola? Did David take a moron pill before he wrote it?

I probably told you that I bought an internal modem for Mom's computer while I was up there, but I didn't have time to install it. I don't think you'd have much of a problem putting it in next time you're there. In fact, it would probably be kind of fun. I haven't done a modem, but I have put in extra memory, which is similar, and it was easy.*

Back then, people often bought bare-bones computers and later opened them up to add memory cards, modems, disk readers, etc.

* * *

Date: 8/8/96
From: Reagan
Subject: Re: That guy in the mirror . . .

Rather intriguing that your message began "If you had one hundred million dollars . . ." as for the past couple of weeks the proposition, "What if I won one hundred million dollars" has been running through my head every day in odd moments. So it was rather disconcerting to get your message. I racked my memory to recall whether I had mentioned this to you, but I don't believe I did. Interesting.*

May I irritate you? The upshot is that winning one hundred million dollars probably wouldn't make my life any happier. I know, I know. That kind of bullshit is irritating. Like the books or movies that try to convince you that if you had three wishes from a genie, it wouldn't really work out. I hate that. Nevertheless, as I run the scenario, I always end up in ungratifying dead ends, like figuring out how much of the money to give away, whether I would buy a Porsche, what I would do with my life, where we would live while raising the kids. It's just not satisfying. I end up just trying to resolve a bunch of troublesome imaginary problems, on top of my own real ones. So it's just not worth it to me. I think I've become a little too self-aware to be able to successfully daydream anymore.

The one exception to the "os" rule: Cheerios. It would be good to eat Cheerios when you're depressed. But not nachos, especially with melted cheese. Taste good going down, but then leave you so heavy and logy.

I love number 2.

Also, many or most computer games. They just suck my mind dry, and suck all the energy out of me too. If I have something to do, and

I sit down to play a couple of games of solitaire first, that's it, I'll get nothing done. I've taken the one-way trolley to zombieville.

I log onto this darn thing just at bedtime, and I never have the time to think much about what I'm writing. I'll have to find a better time. Later, e-mail buddy.

The sharp-eyed reader will note that I had actually mentioned it in my email of 8/4.

* * *

Date: 8/9/96
From: Kevin
Subject: is wearing his lucky undies

I've looked in various men's clothing departments for "lucky rocketship underwear" like Calvin had, but all of the funky designs are on boxers, which I don't find comfortable, except as nightwear. I have one pair of briefs that has a simple abstract design, so I call it my "lucky rocketship underwear" in lieu of the real thing.

Yes, you did briefly mention the one hundred million dollar thing in a previous message. It just seemed to me that the only way to really run as an anti-candidate would be to be self-financed, or to find a wealthy eccentric who liked the idea.

I understand the problems with the fantasy. (You know, it would be interesting to compare fantasies sometime.) I've been through the same things: how to divvy it up, how much money would it take to satisfy all of my desires, how would I manage really big sums of money. The thing is, that kind of fear of money has been a mirror of my real life, a part of my inability to accept and deal with success. These days, I'm dealing a lot better with the ideas of success in general and money in particular. I'm developing the feeling that whatever sums of money come my way, I'll take them gladly and put them to good use, without worrying too much in advance what those uses will be.

Of course, in my current economic state, the first choices are pretty clear: get out of debt, buy a new car, etc. But beyond that, I don't want to let money paralysis present a mental barrier to financial success. I think that the kind of fantasizing you're talking about is detrimental in the usual way of being an unhealthy escape from reality, but it's also particularly damaging in its subject matter. It's "negative visualization." I'm ready to be rich.

* * *

Date: 8/11/96
From: Reagan
Subject: Is responding to multiple messages

Re: David Byrne's liner notes. I have always wanted to be a full-bore Talking Heads/David Byrne fan, as they/he come pretty close to being a group/person I could be a fan of, but I just have never quite been able to do it. I am probably just not capable of being a true fan, because that kind of devotion seems inherently false and self-deceptive to me. True fans seem to have to think that the objects of their devotion are better than humans can really be, and to make them a more important aspect of their lives than anyone who is basically a stranger should be. I think I am just a bit too cold eyed and aware to adopt a true fan mentality. Anyway, stuff like the liner notes you quoted have kept me from successfully deceiving myself into thinking that Byrne is an individual I could elevate to the status of fan-object. I do like their music, but I can't escape the suspicion that if I ever met Byrne, I would find him disappointing and irritating.

I will tackle the internal modem project when I am next in Minot, which should be within the next few weeks.

"Burning Down the House" really is quite satisfying, although I have always wanted one more bout of singing before the end. That is a song that I would like to be able to perform.

So one day, Reagan D, who still has a few leftover pronunciation glitches, was telling me about a really great book he had just read.

August 1996: What Not to do When You're Depressed 231

He said: "You know how good it was Dad?" I said: "How good?" He said: "It walked!"

He meant: "It rocked" of course. I loved it.

I'm fascinated by the fact that you have been seeking lucky rocket ship underwear. It has, out of the blue, kind of made me want them too. Note from the illustrated underwear front: Reagan has always enjoyed underwear with pictures on them. He had Mutant Turtles, Power Rangers, X-Men, Mickey Mouse, many others. Anyway, he has now crossed over the line. This year, he specifically requested plain white underwear, to avoid ribbing from his classmates. So it happens somewhere in the area of second-to-third grade.

I find this rather poignant. Reagan D is a boy of intense interests and strong loyalty. Also, and I know this sounds like a cliche, he is very sensitive. So he finds it hard to abandon the Turtles and the Power Rangers, as his classmates adopt and then abandon each childhood fad and phase with never a backward glance. Reagan really invests himself in those characters, he learns everything about them and enjoys discussing them at great length (and I mean GREAT LENGTH!). He has at times been teased by other boys for still being interested in "baby stuff." It really hurts him. We have explained to him that his brain and his concentration are more powerful than the other boys', and that when they get older they may be able to get as interested in things as he is, and that in the meantime he will have to accept being a little different. But it really breaks my heart. He is so sweet. Why can't childhood be as sweet as my children are? Why have we invented a society in which cruelty and crudeness and deceptiveness and coarseness are admired traits? Why are we so eager to rob our children or their childhoods? Why can't little boys wear underwear and pajamas with pictures on them just as long as they want to?

I'm just so sick of hearing media jerks talk knowingly about "pushing the envelope" and "exploring the dark side" and all that let's-all-just-be-permanent-adolescents-and-worship-nastiness crap. That's a big piece of what Naziism was, you know. A bunch of defective jerks who never really matured past that adolescent phase of thinking that black clothes, and skulls, and daggers, and lightning bolts, and secret symbols were, like, really cool. That's what happened. A bunch of those guys who never made the transition to true maturity ended up running the country, and look what they did. I'll bet they felt really cool the whole time. I hate the whole concept of "cool." What a complete waste of time and effort. But that's what we're doing here in America. Be cool. Dark is good, and true. Wholesome is false and square. Youth and immaturity are cool, the goal is to stay that way forever. THIS IS OUR CULTURE!

As you can see, it's a short way from underwear with pictures on it to a rant against our culture. Of course, for me, it's a short way from any topic to a rant against our culture.

So, I think it's great that you want underwear with rockets.

It's not so much that I'm afraid of money, or that I wouldn't put it to good use. It's just that I've reached the point at which I really know that more money won't give me what I need and want, and that if I had a bunch of it, my life would still involve difficult choices and challenges, and feel quite a bit the same as it does now, except with a lot more goodies in it. So it's not much good as a daydream anymore.

I may be heading for an actual workplace "showdown." This could be interesting. You see this kind of thing on TV and movies, I'm kind of wondering what it might feel like to live through it. The nice thing is, I'm not particularly worried about it. Also, I am still going to look for a win/win everyone-feels-good way to resolve it.

The book "Robinson Crusoe" is very different than I was expecting. I want to find out more about how it was written. Only about the first half take place on the island. I just finished reading a chapter in which Crusoe, now in his 60s and wealthy, is on a trading ship. They stop at Madagascar for supplies, a crewman rapes a native, the natives capture and kill him, and then the crew goes berserk and slaughters about 150 villagers, men, women, and children. Crusoe disapproves, and lectures them so relentlessly that they abandon him in India and sail away. It's pretty intense stuff, but it's all presented in a weirdly low-key fashion. The overall theme of the book is Crusoe continually upbraiding himself for his foolishness and wanderlust, and for his inattention to matters of faith.

* * *

Date: 8/12/96
From: Kevin
Subject: (: = |)

"When I have nothing to say, my lips are sealed." That's not a bad idea, really. It walks.

I agree with you about "Burning Down the House." It's always seemed too short to me.

I, too, feel for Reagan D. Tough to be a sensitive among the barbarians.

Wow. America approaches Naziism culturally, and from the left. Your brain does go places.

Tell me about the showdown. I like the win/win idea. I'm ALWAYS looking for win/win solutions.

I must be remembering "Robinson Crusoe" from Classics Illustrated. The book sounds fascinating.

Come to think of it, The Go-Go's had sealed lips also. I like thinking about their lips better than about David Byrne's.

* * *

Date: 8/12/96
From: Reagan
Subject: Re: (: = |)

I actually use the phrase "when I have nothing to say, my lips are sealed" fairly often. Well, not exactly often. More like from time to time. It is rather interesting, because every once in a while, someone will get a look on his or her face that seems to say: "haven't I heard that somewhere before?" I can't decide whether it's because they actually did hear the song years ago, or because it just sort of sounds like a quote or saying, because of its odd rhythm.

The showdown seems to have evaporated. I'm almost disappointed. We'll have to see, though. If the guy does try to backstab me with the boss, I have many sharp retorts and unpleasant facts at the ready, fully mentally rehearsed. Also, of course my superior attitude of, "I would never get negative like he did because I am a positive team-oriented problem-solving guy, not a devious incompetent weasel like him." Fully rehearsed and 110% genuine.

One interesting thing about "Robinson Crusoe" is that the main character emerges as a sort of bland, self-absorbed, unimaginative plodder. This made him an excellent survivor, but seems to have completely prevented him from experiencing any sense of wonder, or adventure, or excitement. His reactions to the events run the gamut from "this is a horrible ordeal" to "maybe things could be worse, I could be dead." That's about his entire range, right there.

"Say something once, why say it again?"

Those are useful little quotelets. Their later albums don't have that quality. For example I haven't yet been able to work "world moves on a woman's hips, world moves and it bounces and hops" into a conversation yet. Go figure.
More favorites: "And you may ask yourself: well, how did I get here?" And the poignant "My god, what have I done?"

Have you ever said "Same as it ever was" to someone, and then they do the little arm choppy thing from the video right back at you? I did that recently, and it was exquisite.

Nothing satisfies me. "Have you ever had an itch that you just can't scratch?" Yes, as a matter of fact I have you dim witted but powerful homicidal replicant. I eat, it doesn't satisfy. I golf, it doesn't satisfy. I buy stuff, I fish, I work, I everything. It just doesn't ENGAGE me.

How can everyone else get so consumed with these things, so wrapped up in them? How can they enjoy them so much? I know a guy who LOVES to fish! Fishing is fun, but it's just time going by with a little bit going on, in the end. I know a guy who, if he won the lottery, would play golf every day, and he'd be happy. Not only don't these things seem like enough to me, they don't really even seem like much of anything at all. I mean, I'm enjoying golf. It's fun to buy all the gear, and learn all the millions of rules and tips and techniques. But the satisfaction is not deep at all. It's a distraction.

Distraction from what?

* * *

Date: 8/13/96
From: Kevin
Subject: Prodigy sucks

Could you please e-mail my last message back to me? I'm starting to get error messages and system crashes using Prodigy mail, and I only get a partial printout of that message. I apparently don't have a "message sent" queue like you do.

* * *

Date: 8/15/96
From: Kevin
Subject: Unsealed lips

Yes, youth gets smothered and crushed, and adulthood is stunted. Early and lasting adolescence is the rule of the day. Sure, children need to start wising up at some point, start learning some hard truths about the world, but there's a difference between wising up and becoming wiseasses. When what's true and genuine is so quickly and viciously attacked, everything reverts to snide references to something else. I was looking at a display of faux vintage Fossil watches, and suddenly became uncomfortable with the idea that, even in a somewhat benign way, the "wholesomeness batteries" of another era were being sucked dry to fill a void in the present. Anything that has a claim to goodness or purity is either drained or smashed, which I think has a lot to do with the endless fascination with religion in music and videos.

"Adult bookstores." "Adult movies." The only adult things about them is the chronological age of the customers. What does the truly adult world, the world of maturity, have to offer as a step beyond the hyperkinetic symbolism of today's popular culture? Adults today are relegated to being old teenagers, or threatened with being assigned the roles of '50s-style caricatures.

"Fully rehearsed and 110% genuine." What a great phrase.

I've never had the "same as it ever was" experience in quite that way, although with Peggy and the McManuses it has been a part of conversation ever since the video came out.

Nothing satisfies you, not even fishing? You'll probably end up in Scientology. "Hey, Kev, now I feel satisfied ALL THE TIME! Plus, I'm making twenty million dollars a picture now! You should try it."

And, speaking of Travolta, what's with the media obsession with weight? I think he looks GREAT with more weight, and I think it's worked to his advantage in his recent roles. Would skinny John have been believable in "Get Shorty"? Alicia Silverstone put on a few pounds after "Clueless," and when she was signed to play Batgirl, one of the tabloid headlines was "Look out Batman! Here comes Buttgirl!" That's an immoral message, bordering on the criminal, to be spreading to today's young women. I've seen similar pounding on Richard Gere, Denzel Washington and one of the Baywatch women.

* * *

Date: 8/16/96
From: Reagan
Subject: Re: Unsealed lips

I hadn't quite thought of it that way, although I guess I had seen both sides of it. I knew that on one hand, our culture seems determined to end childhood as quickly as possible, and basically tells kids they should be "street smart" adolescent wiseasses by age 6. And I knew that on the other hand our culture strongly tells us that we should never grow up, that maturity isn't "cool" and that "cool" is of supreme importance. But your message really hit the point, which is obvious but still struck me as fresh and important: that these are two sides of the same phenomenon, which is that we are supposed to be in adolescence for our entire conscious lives. Which is ironic, since adolescence is the most repulsive and unpleasant stage of life.

Also a real bell ringer on the way we are draining our wholesomeness batteries. We have mocked and undermined and rebelled against absolutely every darn thing, to the point, as we have both noticed in recent years, that we are now making up fake stuff, or delving way back into a sort of caricature '50s, to "rebel" against or mock. Doesn't everyone get it? There's nothing left! Rebellion and cynicism ARE the establishment. Maturity and wholesomeness are subversive and individualistic! The only TV show that could truly "push the envelope" not would be one in which the protagonists are deeply religious.

This weight thing is a crock. I'm better looking now than I ever was when I was thin, and hey, that's saying a lot! I agree that the Silverstone thing was an outrage. I generally don't give a rip about celebrity media coverage, but that one really steamed me. Those people should be ritually humiliated.

Have you seen "Clueless?" It's a must rent. She's excellent!

I already bought a Christmas gift for you. My life is so much more organized than it used to be in so many ways. I really do have a strong feeling that I am now travelling much more efficiently and effectively on the "road of life," although, of course, I have absolutely no idea where I am going. In circles, most likely. Or big crazy loopy ellipses. I'm fairly confident I am not travelling in rectangles, or rhombuses, or anything else with sharp corners. I'd prefer not to think of myself as travelling in a spiral, in which I revisit the same points in life but on progressively higher planes, because that would be painfully trite in a sort of sophomoric pseudo-philosophic way.

For a number of years I thought that Jeff Goldblum and Harold Ramis were the same person. There are two or three big beefy actors with light hair that I have the same problem with.

* * *

Date: 8/18/96
From: Kevin
Subject: (: =>)

Hey, I already bought a Christmas gift for me, too, so big deal.

It's possible that you're travelling along the boundary of the Mandelbrot set. Look into it.

Is Gary Busey one of them?

New topic: Good things about life in the Nineties.

> 24-hour supermarkets
>
> Pay-at-the-pump gas stations
> Debit cards
>
> E-mail

Things that are mostly good:

> Less and less gender stereotyping (Upside: freedom. Downside: role confusion)
>
> Computer-aided special effects (Great when used properly, as in Terminator II or Forrest Gump. Annoying when used ineptly, as in Species – especially at the end – or when you can tell that they've thrown in some morphing more because they can do it than because it fits or looks good – which happens all too frequently.)

***

Date: 8/18/96
From: Kevin
Subject: is nodding off

What do you take for allergy-related tiredness besides your Bizarro version of coffee? I've been feeling a particular kind of sleepiness lately that I suspect is related to my seasonal allergies.

It's interesting to observe different kinds of tiredness in myself. This sleepiness feels druglike, like the "drowsiness" that medication labels warn about. Other types of tiredness: Simple lack-of-sleep, tiredness from physical exertion, mental fatigue, and depressive lethargy (related to emotional tiredness).

There have been a few occasions recently where I was getting by happily and productively with very little sleep, except that I was apparently not dreaming enough! It seemed as though dreams would start even before I was fully asleep.

A particularly pleasant form of sleepiness (when it can be indulged, anyway) is the siesta sort, the kind that can be satisfied by a 20-to-60-minute nap in the late afternoon. Dad used to nap when he came home from work, remember? Interesting.

***

Date: 8/24/96
From: Reagan
Subject: object, predicate, verb

Two of the beefy blonde actors I have a hard time keeping straight are Brian Keith and Brian Dennehy. I think there might be a third, but I don't know for sure, BECAUSE I CAN'T KEEP THEM STRAIGHT!

Amen to your four "good things about the '90s." More nominees:

American cars

Uglier teen clothing than we wore (thereby lifting the onus)

No cold war/children raised without threat of nuclear annihilation (my kids are intrigued and puzzled to think that we recently had a powerful enemy and that we threatened to blow each other up)

Cheap gas (relatively speaking)

Yeah, morphing is great, except in those clumsy movies when you have a scene setting up a morphing shot and it's like there's a huge neon sign flashing "here comes the morph, pay attention, this was 25% of the whole damn budget."

I take Seldane (oral) and Nasacort (in the schnozz) from about May 1 until the first hard frost, morning and night. Remainder of the year: morning only. I have recently received propaganda telling me Claritin is better than Seldane, so I may experiment, after consulting my doctor.

Ah yes, nap sleepiness. A pleasure right up there with taking a good dump, or being real thirsty, and having ready access to tasty liquids. I love napping. But, as you say, it has to be the right sleepiness at the right time.

Here is the first sentence of "Far from the Madding Crowd" by Thomas Hardy:

> When Farmer Oak smiled, the corners of his mouth spread till they were within an unimportant distance of his ears, his eyes were reduced to chinks, and diverging wrinkles appeared round them, extending upon his countenance like the rays in a rudimentary sketch of the rising sun.

I was so struck by this sentence, that I put the book down, resolving not to read it until I had at least an hour to devote to it, as this sentence seemed to promise a book so skillfully written, that I would not want to read it in snatches and pieces, but in long stretches, so that I could be drawn into it.

* * *

Date: 8/29/96
From: Kevin
Subject:

Thanks for the phone calls. Very invigorating.

More good things about the Nineties:

    Big bookstores with coffee shops

    No-smoking zones everywhere

    Speed limits going back up

    Cheap, disposable contacts

That's a heck of a first sentence. Let me know how it is after that.

13. September 1996: The Hulk

Date: 9/4/96
From: Kevin
Subject:

I went to an allergist and am now using a nasal spray. I'm also trying a few different oral medications, including Claritin. My allergy symptoms, including the sleepiness, are much improved. This is certainly a pathetic little note, but it's all I have to say.

* * *

Date: 9/8/96
From: Reagan
Subject: My own private Idaho

Here are my concise but sincere replies:

Thanks for the New Yorkers. I found them intellectually stimulating. Reading them made me feel somewhat reawakened and refreshed. I believe I will subscribe.

No-smoking areas are perhaps the very best thing about the '90s.

You had some good ones there. The contacts were great, and the speed limits too. It's like playing the '70s in rewind: better cars, cheap gas, higher cruising speeds. Too bad those horrible '70s clothing designs have returned.

Glad to hear the allergy thing is working out.

I'm kinda flat here, and I haven't been communicating much, because things are in full meltdown.

If I didn't start out nuts, I'm well on my way there. These last couple weeks, I have felt close to losing my grip in a big way. I'm sleep walking through work. It doesn't help that we're having a ferocious allergy season here, and that half the time I'm operating with the focused intelligence of a kumquat. I thought I had laid a nice foundation in my life that I could build on, and now it's all melting away.

* * *

Date: 9/10/96
From: Kevin
Subject:

I seem to have misplaced my ability to write interesting or amusing notes. Not a concern, but an irritation.

Let's go huntin'.

* * *

Date: 9/13/96
From: Kevin
Subject:

Well, we're heading out for a few days in Minneapolis. We're staying at a bed-and-breakfast in Stillwater tonight, and with Tom tomorrow.

Glad to hear that things are a little calmer there. I'll call when we get back.

* * *

Date: 9/18/96
From: Kevin
Subject:

We stayed with Tom last Saturday night, in the room of his ten-year-old son, John. John had the usual sort of boy-stuff up on his door, including one item that I liked so much that I asked to have it (John consented). It was a handmade sign, done in yellow and black crayon. In the middle was a radiation symbol, and below it was this:

WARING!
DO NOT ENTER!
Toxic Ridation!

Not much else. Received a couple of encouraging rejection letters.

Still fighting this bug. How's the tooth situation?*

*Reagan had the disconcerting experience of having a front tooth fall out while eating a turkey leg at a street fair. Of course, it took several months to have it replaced with an implant – which was new dental technology at that time – and the temporary replacement tooth made his speaking voice mushy. As a result, he had to give quite a few speeches with a gap in his smile. He managed the situation by turning it into a humorous rapport-builder with audiences.

* * *

Date: 9/20/96
From: Kevin
Subject: Box

The Atlantic article on city planning was a rare one in that I mentally questioned nearly everything I read, without just tossing the whole thing aside in irritation. I felt challenged, invigorated, and enlightened, the way you're supposed to when reading something controversial. The difference was that it seemed constructively controversial, rather than the far too common versions of pot-stirring, naysaying, and whining.

The wings are a bit tattered, but Emily thought that Sabrina might like them.

I'm not sure why I have this minor fascination with the future of Saudi Arabia, but I'm surprised that they're already in such bad shape. I'll probably have more to say later.

The other stuff is self-explanatory.

* * *

Date: 9/25/96
From: Kevin
Subject:

Absinthe bakes the tart crow fondue.

* * *

Date: 9/26/96
From: Kevin
Subject: HULK WILL SMASH!

I remember being in the little corner grocery store near our house in Minot, and looking at the rack of comic books that was at the end of one of the checkout aisles. One cover in particular impressed me: the Hulk struggling uphill against the power beam of some forgotten foe. I thought of that cover over the years, intrigued by the idea of exerting such tremendous effort against a great force. I wondered if I really had it in me to be in that kind of situation and not give up.

I thought of it again a while ago, and realized, of course, that I HAD fought that fight, battling uphill against the Depress-o-beam. Felt pretty good about that.

* * *

Date: 9/28/96
From: Reagan
Subject: Re: HULK WILL SMASH!

Unfortunately, it appears I'm Ant Man.

***

Date: 9/30/96
From: Kevin
Subject: Ant Reag

As I recall, we would have been more than pleased to have had Ant Man's powers when we were kids.

From a newspaper article on Kuwait:

> "The Kuwaiti, he does not like to work," said Falah al-Rashidi, a 23-year-old Kuwaiti assigned to the National Guard. "The foreigners have experience that we lack, and they work for lower salaries. This does not mean that the Kuwaiti does not contribute. But this way the Kuwaiti can stay safe and rested."

From a New Yorker profile of Yip Harburg, who wrote the lyrics for "Somewhere Over the Rainbow" and "Brother Can You Spare a Dime?":

> What Harburg heard [when he listened to rock music] was the death rattle of the culture. "They communicate only emotional intensity. They're crude. It upsets me" he said. "You're living in a savage world, and when you listen to the shrieks and savage cries in the songs you know it." He added, "Songs now are a reflection of fright. It's the fright of no hope, no stability. When we began writing songs, we felt that life was good. The world was beautiful, and we were enjoying it. Death was at the end of the adventure, but we didn't worry about that. These kids are worried. They're on their deathbeds, and they're teen-agers!"

I'll send you both pieces soon.

14. October 1996: Emotional Chrysalis

Date: 10/10/96
From: Kevin
Subject:

Saw "Fargo," and enjoyed it. Not a great movie, but a lot of resonance for me – the people, the places, the weather, the attitudes. Sure, the accents were a little overdone, but other linguistic regions probably get the same treatment – think about the New England accents you hear in the media and the way our generation of Maine relatives actually sounds.

Man, I can sure remember feeling like Lundegaard – the hideous mountain of internalized anxiety, the sure things falling through at the last minute, the desperation, the insanity. Of course, now I just have a cup of coffee and I'm fine. Nyuk nyuk.

I'm wondering – do you ever see in me the kind of glittery peppiness that seems to be the hallmark of ex-head cases? The women tend to be to chipper, and the men have a kind of forced joviality. I will have myself beaten, if necessary, to erase such behavior.

***

Date: 10/12/96
From: Reagan
Subject: Re: No Subject

I'm emerging from some kind of emotional chrysalis here. You know I think I may have just been through some kind of cumulative reaction to a long series of hard to handle experiences. As I wrote that sentence, it suddenly made a lot of sense to me that I've been having a bit of a hard time lately. I would really like an emotional break here. Prolonged uneventfulness would be nice.

Now that I'm emerging from my chrysalis, I'm horrified to discover that I have huge gauzy multi-colored wings! How will I explain THIS at the office!

I want to contribute, while staying safe and well-rested. And incredibly rich and oblivious. What an interesting choice of words: "safe and well-rested." Some kind of cultural value on being well-rested?

Yip Harburg has a perspective on life that we are sorely lacking, nowadays.

You aren't an ex-head case, and you don't act like one. At all.

Yeah, that trapped rat in the corner thing that the Lundgaard character had going in "Fargo" hit way too close to home for me. I did enjoy the movie, though.

I wish you were here so much that all evening I've been catching myself listening for your voice.

Afterword

Kevin: The emails go on, of course, but this first burst of online conversation is a unique window into both the state of our lives at the time and the birth of a new technology. Within a few years I would learn HTML and publish what was then called an "e-zine" that included fiction, cartoons, movie reviews, and a blog on dealing with depression.

Reagan: I left the Bureau after five years and moved my family to Omaha to be in the same city with Kevin and his family. In 2000, Kevin and I, along with our mother Sally, formed SKR Pufall, a company focused on public speaking and publishing. Kevin and I wrote and self-published Solution Power, a self-help problem solving guide, and launched a speaking career based on the material. That ended when my unintended career as a business executive took off after I joined a young company that grew rapidly and was acquired by Berkshire Hathaway. I am currently the CEO of Omaha National, an insurance company I co-founded in 2016.

Kevin: When our speaking career ended I pursued several interests, including modeling and acting. I'm now back to writing.

www.ingramcontent.com/pod-product-compliance
Lightning Source LLC
LaVergne TN
LVHW051546070426
835507LV00021B/2437